Praise for *And Th...*

"In this funny, insightful book, Rachel ....sks hard questions and actually comes up with some answers. It's a must read for everyone who struggles to find a path, fulfill their potential, make a living, and make a life." —Emily Gould, author of *Friendship*

"*And Then We Grew Up* is real as hell and made me feel so seen. Friedman captures so perfectly the endless quest to be a functional happy person in the world who is also, somehow, an art monster. Searching, honest, and generous, this book is a consoling and revealing meditation on making peace with your life."
—Meaghan O'Connell, author of *And Now We Have Everything*

"Advice about doing what you love often clashes with reality in midlife. In her thoughtful, generous book—a kind of *The Big Chill* reckoning for mid-life creatives—Rachel Friedman explores how she and her talented childhood friends reached various states of disillusionment and fulfillment. *And Then We Grew Up* is the perfect gift for anyone trying to reconcile a desire to write, play music, or make art with more pedestrian desires, like having a family, food on the table, or peace of mind."
—Ada Calhoun, author of *Wedding Toasts I'll Never Give*

"Did you grow up pointed in an artistic direction? Did you not, but wonder about those who did? Do you have kids of your own with art in their hearts? If yes on any of those, *And Then We Grew Up* will be of interest on a dozen levels. With candor and humor and perfect intonation, Rachel Friedman gets at one of the biggest questions of all: What *happens* to us as we get older?"
—Chris Colin, author of *What to Talk About* and *What Really Happened to the Class of '93*

"An insightful, informative, and unexpectedly heartfelt look at all of the ways in which art touches our lives. Friedman reminds us that even if we hang up our dance shoes, neglect our paint set, or box up our musical instruments, creativity never really leaves us."

—Geraldine DeRuiter, author of *All Over the Place: Adventures in Travel, True Love, and Petty Theft*

"In *And Then We Grew Up*, Rachel Friedman is a wise and funny guide through a tangle of hard questions about art, work, and life— about what it means to 'make it,' about the many shades of success and failure, and about the search for fulfillment through creativity. Brave enough to examine her own biases, assumptions, and hangups, she provides a way forward for the rest of us who have wrestled with these questions, too. Essential reading for anyone who wonders about the role of creativity and art in their life."

—Eva Holland, author of *Nerve: Adventures in the Science of Fear*

PENGUIN BOOKS

AND THEN WE GREW UP

Rachel Friedman is the author of *And Then We Grew Up* and *The Good Girl's Guide to Getting Lost*. Her work has appeared in *The Best Women's Travel Writing*, *The McSweeney's Book of Politics and Musicals*, *The New York Times*, *Creative Nonfiction*, and *The Chronicle of Higher Education*, among others. She lives in Brooklyn with her son.

ALSO BY RACHEL FRIEDMAN

The Good Girl's Guide to Getting Lost

And Then We Grew Up

ON CREATIVITY, POTENTIAL, AND THE
IMPERFECT ART OF ADULTHOOD

Rachel Friedman

PENGUIN BOOKS

PENGUIN BOOKS
An imprint of Penguin Random House LLC
penguinrandomhouse.com

LIBRARY OF CONGRESS CATALOGING-IN-PUBLICATION DATA

Names: Friedman, Rachel, 1981– author.
Title: And then we grew up : on creativity, potential, and the imperfect
art of adulthood / Rachel Friedman.
Description: New York : Penguin Books, [2019] |
Includes bibliographical references.
Identifiers: LCCN 2019019646 (print) | LCCN 2019020365 (ebook) |
ISBN 9780525503859 (ebook) | ISBN 9780143132127 (paperback)
Subjects: LCSH: Friedman, Rachel, 1981– |
Women authors—United States—Biography. | Adulthood. |
Conduct of life. | Self-actualization (Psychology)
Classification: LCC CT275.F714 (ebook) | LCC CT275.F714 A3 2020 (print) |
DDC 305.24—dc23
LC record available at https://lccn.loc.gov/2019019646

Printed in the United States of America
1   3   5   7   9   10   8   6   4   2

BOOK DESIGN BY LUCIA BERNARD

For Eben

AUTHOR'S NOTE

I have changed most names in this book. Conversations and texts have been edited for length and clarity, and some time frames have been compressed. However, all melodramatic, existential despair of mine described in these pages is entirely unaltered.

"History," said Wah, sipping his beer. "We are constantly living the history of our own lives, you dig? You used to be your old self, now you're a new self, and someday you'll be some other self and what's now will be your old self . . . History! Don't sweat It."

—Laurie Colwin, *Goodbye Without Leaving*

CONTENTS

And Then
We Grew Up

1

Potential

This all started with taxes. I had taken the E train out to the last stop in Queens and descended a few crumbling steps into my accountant's drab basement office. Every year I seemed to interrupt him in the middle of lunch, no matter the hour of our appointment, and this visit was no exception. His right hand deftly directed chopsticks full of sesame chicken into his mouth while his left tapped numbers into a computer. *In a different life*, the former musician part of my brain thought, *he might have made a decent pianist.*

I had made barely enough money that year to cover rent and groceries, but I reasoned that *barely* was pretty good in Manhattan, an increasingly unaffordable borough for artists who once thrived there. I had taken on any and every freelance writing assignment, from churning out SEO clickbait for travel websites to "reporting" on heat-resistant makeup for a glossy women's food mag. I'd become a veritable pitching machine, developing into overdrive the *Minority Report* part of one's brain capable of scanning every new person, place, and piece of news for a potential story angle.

Nevertheless, when my accountant added up the numbers, I somehow owed way more money than was in my savings account, which was more of an aspirational idea than a place actual currency resided.

"Four thousand dollars," he said through a mouthful of Chinese food.

"Four thousand?" I gasped.

"Four thousand," he said, swallowing.

FOUR. THOUSAND. DOLLARS. The impossible number kept echoing in my head as I wandered back toward the subway. My West Fourth Street stop let me off by IFC, my favorite cinema, and I heard my film professor father's voice telling me that the best escape from my anxiety was right there in front of me. I bought a ticket for a movie whose poster gave off a *Bonnie and Clyde* vibe and settled into the nearly empty theater.

At first my film cure worked. I was distracted by the young lovers' troubled relationship and their hypnotic southern drawls. By the gunfight scene, I was in another world entirely, one where money was made by stealin' and nobody owed the government a goddamn cent. But then a handsome sheriff appeared on-screen.

"Just sit tight a little longer," he told the doe-eyed protagonist.

I leaned forward, trying to place the familiar-looking actor as he tipped his cowboy hat and shuffled mustache-first out of the woman's ramshackle house. Though he was the strong, silent type, it was obvious from the way he looked at her that he was in love. But there was another man (a dangerous man!) and a young daughter in the picture complicating matters.

What had I seen him in before? My mind flipped through its movie Rolodex for a few seconds before I realized the serious sheriff was the same wisecracking kid I had known twenty years ago at Interlochen, an intense performing arts camp for kids ages eight through eighteen in northern Michigan. I went there for music, but other campers were actors, dancers, and visual artists.

This déjà vu moment happened every three or four years when I randomly caught Ben in a movie or on TV. He had been an exceptionally good actor even back when we were kids in a place where unformed talent permeated every humid camp cabin. We all knew when we saw him onstage that it was only a matter of time before he made it. Now thirty-three, Ben was an actor's actor respected by even the orneriest critics. He was one mainstream breakout role away from becoming a household celebrity name.

His success had never bothered me before. Why should it? He was an actor who lived in a dreamy, moneyed, faraway land called Hollywood that had nothing to do with my pursuing music as a kid or creative writing as an adult. I had always delighted in catching glimpses of him over the years, but in that post-taxes moment, I had the gut-punch realization of just how far our artistic paths had diverged. There he was, larger than life, talented and successful. He had spun all that early potential into a brilliant career. And here I was, wrist deep in greasy popcorn, wondering how to pay off this debt of mine.

Interlochen

I started viola lessons when I was eight and loved playing from the moment I picked my instrument out of a school auditorium lineup of more-coveted violins and cellos.

"Rachel has demonstrated outstanding ability in every way on the viola," my music teacher wrote on my first report card. "She has a great ear, excellent coordination, and a spirit that never quits. She is a very 'bright light' in my day." To the left of the "Excellent" column Mrs. B. had handwritten in an extra "Outstanding" column and put Xs in all three categories: "mastery of technical skill," "effort," and "development of responsibility." She told my parents I was "a natural."

I'm sure learning how to play viola must have been awkward at first: balancing an hourglass-shaped piece of wood between my chin and shoulder, figuring out the right amount of bow pressure to avoid squeaking, teaching my fingers the unforgivingly specific coordinates of each individual note. But what I remember most is feeling an immediate, deep connection to my instrument, a sense that we were a perfect fit. I remember the feeling of falling in love.

BEFORE CAMP, I coasted along on natural ability, high on the gold-star stickers my music teacher bestowed each time

I mastered a new song. I quickly outpaced the other kids at my school, but it wasn't until my first summer at Interlochen that I understood how much talent was out there in the world. Suddenly I was surrounded by truly phenomenal musicians, kids who practiced hours a day. The camp stoked in my eleven-year-old self an ambition to achieve musical greatness.

Interlochen was built on the premise of potential. Joseph Maddy, its founder, envisioned it as a place for America's untapped creative youth. It was initially a camp solely for musicians, but after a decade or so it expanded to include dance, acting, and the visual arts. A dancer's day at Interlochen is filled with hours of ballet, modern, and jazz classes. When I was there, the theater majors put on twelve to sixteen plays in eight weeks, including sewing period costumes, building elaborate sets, and nurturing future divas. Those who came for the visual arts studied ceramics, drawing, painting, printmaking, and photography. Their new work was exhibited every week. We musicians spent our days in auditions, orchestra rehearsals, sectionals, and private lessons, and if you were Serious, you sweltered several hours a day in one of the muggy practice huts scattered around the 1,200-acre pinewoods-covered campus. There were six auditoriums and around five hundred performances throughout the summer. The camp was (and still is) boot camp for creative kids. It's where my friends and I learned just how committed we were to our callings.

Interlochen was governed by strict routines and rituals: classes, rehearsals, and practice hours at the same time each day. A bugle woke us up with reveille at 6:40 A.M. and sent us off to bed each evening with taps at 9:15 P.M. We did "capers" every morning after announcements—sweeping the steps, making our beds, *scrubbing the toilets*. We wore uniforms six days of the week: blue shirts, blue shorts or corduroy knickers, and color-coded blue or red socks and belts designating our division: junior, intermediate, or high school. Tie a flannel around your waist, throw on some Doc Martens or Birkenstocks, and don't forget your name badge and Walkman. The camp embraced a Flaubertian philosophy of art: "Be regular and orderly in your life . . . so that you may be violent and original in your work."

Interlochen is where I learned to practice. My parents early on instilled in me that practice was important. When I begged to start the guitar at age six, they made clear I needed to play for fifteen minutes a day: butt in chair, no excuses. But Interlochen is where I really cultivated discipline. It is where I learned that an artist is always and forever practicing, that practice is the thread connecting one day to the next. I found this repetition liberating versus confining. Every morning I woke up knowing exactly what I needed to do.

As a shy, angsty preteen, the only time I felt completely present and at ease in my body was when I was playing viola. My childhood friends had become the popular middle school clique and halfheartedly dragged me along with them. But I existed mostly on the periphery, where my precarious spot at the lunch table was forever in jeopardy should I make one false move. At home, my parents'

unhappy marriage was imploding at an excruciatingly gla-
cial pace, so I was on guard there, too, constantly gauging
their moods and doing my best to keep them happy. But
when I played the viola, I felt confident and powerful and
free. I could let everything else go and disappear into the
music.

At camp, I was suddenly able to embody this state of creative freedom and self-expression 24/7. An example: I remember our little clique of friends loudly singing and acting
out the "Jet Song" from *West Side Story*. The theater kids
among us had started it off, but the dancers and musicians
joined right in. We snapped our fingers, swaggering, stomp-
ing, and belting our way through the campus. Every time
we passed a new group of kids, they would sing along with
us. I would *never* have been so boisterously, nerdily, enthusiastically musical back home.

I wanted to feel that free all the time, and I associated
freedom with becoming an artist. And who was an artist?
She was fiercely talented, ambitious, and uncompromising.
She bucked convention. Her emotions were deep and profound, and the world clamored for her to share them.

These were the qualities nurtured in us at camp. We were
encouraged to be bold. To experiment. To have vision and
passion. I observed these traits in my friends: confident actors, emotive ballerinas, intense musicians, and thoughtful
painters. And then there were the famous musicians who
came to perform at Interlochen. I saw the bassist Edgar
Meyer, the cellist Yo-Yo Ma, the violinist Isaac Stern, and the
Emerson String Quartet. I saw Aretha Franklin, the Indigo

Girls, Emmylou Harris, Bobby McFerrin, Willie Nelson, and Ray Charles. I wanted to be up on that stage one day, too.

At camp, I began to hone a vision of my future musician's life. I loved chamber music and pictured myself forming a string quartet at music school. After graduating, we'd travel all over the world for gigs, winning competitions and selling out concert halls, periodically returning to the United States to play Carnegie Hall. Strangers in whatever foreign city I happened to be in would see me crossing their streets with my scuffed viola case or marking up my sheet music on the train or would notice the red mark under the left side of my jaw where the skin was rubbed raw from practicing. And they would know instantly who I was: a musician living her beautiful, adventurous, creative life. Back then, all of this seemed to be not only within reach but the inevitable outcome of hard work and big ambition.

From a very early age, then, I had a Path. I knew exactly where I wanted to go in life and the necessary steps to get there, and I was positive I knew how deeply satisfying it would be once I arrived.

Not that I made it. Not by a long shot.

MY POST-INTERLOCHEN artistic path had taken more detours than my film actor former campmate's had. I continued to excel in music—for a while. I was often first chair in all-county and then in all-state orchestras, and in my local youth symphony. Until high school, when I decided to focus exclusively on viola, I took guitar and piano lessons as well. I took composition lessons. I sang in the Syracuse Children's Chorus. I was in all of my school's musicals, beginning at age ten with what my father to this day still insists was a "brilliantly nuanced" performance as the White Rabbit in *Alice in Wonderland*. Music was most definitely "my bag," as the writer Meghan Daum efficiently put it.

In college, though, everything changed. Off I went to study with the principal violist of the Boston Symphony, but I buckled almost immediately under the pressure of our intense lessons and the reality check that I was no longer even close to The Best. At Interlochen, it had mostly been older kids who were better than me, but of the three freshman viola performance majors in my program, I was the weakest. I spent four hours a day practicing, but I just couldn't get better fast enough. In fact, the more anxious I was to improve, the worse I seemed to get.

Once a week I'd call my dad sobbing, unable to explain exactly why I was so overwhelmed and miserable doing the thing I had loved for as long as I could remember. I'd wake in a panic at two or three A.M. most mornings, the panic softening into dread as I watched the minutes tick by. Every hour of every day was a countdown to my weekly private lesson. I would start to feel nauseous the night before. If I was lucky, I'd only lose my appetite, but often on the day of my lesson I found myself kneeling on grungy bathroom tiles, throwing up whatever cafeteria food I'd managed to get down for breakfast.

My friend Jane would sometimes knock on the door. "Are you okay?"

"Uh-huh," I'd mumble. "I just need a minute."

I could see her black Steve Madden boots through the gap at the bottom of the door. I'd zone in on them like a seasick person would on the horizon. I'd breathe in and out, eventually pulling myself together. That first semester I became almost unhinged by stress and unhappiness and lack of sleep; a mere three months of music school was enough to suck all the joy from playing.

The long afternoons I spent in those basement practice rooms mostly blur together in an emotional arc from determined to frustrated to desperate, but I do have a distinct memory of the morning I knew I was really in trouble. I had warmed up with some scales. Next up was a Kreutzer étude. I had it open on my music stand. I put my bow down for a minute to drink some water, and when I picked it up again, I felt that no matter how I adjusted my fingers, they were in the wrong place. My grip was awkward, shaky. I squeaked across the strings, like a beginner. And I just couldn't get comfortable again no matter what I tried. The relentless deconstructing and rebuilding of my technique that musicians often undergo with new teachers as they advance had made me too hyperaware of every movement.

In that moment, I fought the sudden urge to break my bow in half. *What a relief that would be,* I thought. *Just break it and be done once and for all.* Instead, I put my instrument in its case and shakily backed away.

I knew music school was supposed to weed people out. I'd just assumed it would be *other* weeds. And certainly not that I'd be the first to get yanked from the garden. I quit viola before the end of my freshman year. Halfway through sophomore year, I transferred to another university in a different city. I declared myself all washed up at the tender age of nineteen, directionless, purposeless, *ordinary*—now just one of the scores of young adults trying to figure out what to do when they grow up. Looking back, I can see that part of what hit me so hard was being disabused of the naive belief that my plan for my adult life would work out exactly as I had envisioned it. It requires having an absurdly charmed childhood to lose your innocence this way at nineteen, but there you have it.

Still, I never fully stopped daydreaming about what my life might have been like if I'd never put down my bow. Even in my thirties I still imagined performing onstage. Or I'd hear, say, Bach's Cello Suite no. 1 in a restaurant, a piece I'd played a thousand times, and find myself drawn back into those long, slurred bows, lost in the music while a dinner date wondered where I'd gone. I'd awkwardly hedge whenever someone from my past asked if I still played viola. "Not as much as I'd like to" was my usual noncommittal response, when the true answer was "hardly ever." Some part of me really did believe that any day now I would start practicing again, that my old musician's life still existed in some parallel universe, a Narnia just waiting for me to walk through the wardrobe.

From Music to Writing

Still feeling lost after graduation, I decided to get more lost by backpacking and waitressing my way around the world for a few years. I wanted to put an ocean between me and the question on every adult's lips: "So what's next?"

While I was traveling, I turned to writing to help me make sense of feeling adrift and to document my backpacking adventures. I had been a lonely bookworm kid, the kind who stayed up way too late reading under her covers and never cared about being sent to her room as a form of punishment because that's where all the *books* were. Writing had been a private creative pursuit since I could string words into sentences. In middle school, I'd fill journal after journal with scavenged dialogue—overheard fights between my parents or boys' inane school-bus chatter. I wrote little plays. I wrote a *lot* of bad poetry. In high school, I started writing essays and short stories. In college, I kept this up and occasionally showed my work to friends or teachers.

I suppose it makes sense that when I quit viola, writing moved in to fill the creative hole it left. While I was traveling, I unconsciously transferred my musician's discipline to writing, carving out time each day to describe raucous Irish bars, Australian ghost towns abandoned after drought and dust storms, and death-defying bus rides through Bolivian mountains, as well as all the ordinary details of daily life suddenly re-enchanted because I was experiencing them far from home. By the time I returned to the States, I was determined to pour my energies into professionalizing this other creative passion.

I don't know when exactly I linked the private act of writing to more slippery ideas of what it meant to be a Writer, but it happened somewhere along the way, just as it had with music. I fantasized about signing one book contract after another, filling my expansive days with writing and research and my nights with wine-filled gatherings of the literary elite. I'd spend my summers at MacDowell or Bread Loaf, and every few years teach a workshop at whichever prestigious university had successfully courted me as a writer in residence. I'd go on book tours, where I'd read to adoring crowds. As with music, I believed that all of this and more was up for grabs if I just worked hard enough.

While I was falling in love with writing and traveling, I also fell in *love* love. I met a robustly bearded New Zealander, whom I'll call P, in an Irish bar in Peru. He seduced me that first night by outlining an invisible map of his country on my arm.

"Here's Auckland," he said, pointing to my index finger. "Wellington, Christchurch." By the time he reached Invercargill at the bend in my elbow, I was a goner.

I was only twenty-five when we got married—practically a child bride in the eyes of my incredulous New York friends, although no one was more shocked than me. A child of divorce who aspired to be an untethered Bohemian artist, I'd never intended to marry young, if at all.

But when push came to green card, getting married seemed like a brilliant idea both romantically and logistically. Soon I sold my first book. *Only twenty-six*, I inwardly crowed, *and already I'm a Real Writer.*

I have a frozen-in-time image of myself in this seemingly perfect moment. I had a book contract. The love of a good man. A rent-controlled apartment. I remember thinking that I had really nailed this whole being-an-adult thing, but one of adulthood's most powerful life lessons is how fleeting a moment can be.

My So-Called Artistic Life

That a first "big break" is the start of one's inevitable upward trajectory is of course the fantasy of the uninitiated writer, and *ohhhhh*, how I indulged it. I would have done so to some extent even without P, but with his salary at an advertising agency as a safety net, we decided I should quit my editorial assistant job to work on the book. I naively assumed that publishing a book meant I would seamlessly transition into forever making my living from writing.

By my early thirties, I had accomplished some of what I had set out to do. I'd published a book and carved out a freelance career. I'd taught writing classes. I'd won a prize here, had an essay anthologized there. I did indeed drink wine. Yet I was constantly attuned to all the ways I fell short of my own lofty expectations.

I'd published a first book, but my second book had been rejected, my former editor explaining she just couldn't convince the middle-aged men running her marketing team to get excited about a "first chapter on periods." (I'll leave you in suspense about whether my proposal unsuccessfully attempted to illuminate punctuation or pregnancy.) I wasn't an esteemed professor but instead had held various low-paying adjunct and summer positions. The prize was a small one. The anthology wasn't the best one. I had a circle of wonderful writer and editor friends, but I certainly hadn't been invited over to Gay Talese's for a bottle of Cabernet, and I wasn't holding my breath for his call.

I knew I was being too hard on myself for not achieving the artistic greatness I'd envisioned and also truly believed I was failing to live up to my potential. I'm embarrassed to admit how hard and late the epiphany hit that no one but my father was earnestly awaiting my next piece of writing. That not only was I probably never going to be canonized alongside writers I revered, but I was older than pretty much every Victorian poet I had loved in college was when they died. When they *died*.

These feelings were familiar.

Much as I had once loved music, I loved writing, but the way I felt about writing had over time become infected with anxiety and self-doubt. Just as had been true with music, I'd enjoyed some early successes with writing, which left me believing that everything after those points would be smooth sailing—a belief that was inevitably followed by an accompanying sense of disappointment when my achievements didn't continue in an uninterrupted linear path. Once again, I had thought I would be an outlier success story, and instead I was flailing around in the middle of the pack.

"Would it really be *so bad* if you only ever wrote one book?" a friend tipsily inquired over drinks one night as I was lamenting all this.

"You mean, would complete and utter failure be so bad?" I said, doing a spot-on impression of the melodramatic nineteen-year-old Rachel who had wandered aimlessly around campus after her viola dreams were crushed.

Unlike what had happened with music, I wasn't considering quitting writing, but I didn't know how much of my living I could really expect to make from it, and I very badly wanted it to be a career, not a hobby. My identity as a writer felt so fragile, like someone could just snatch it away if I wasn't holding on tightly enough. Increasingly I felt disappointed and discontented, and I worried about these feelings hardening into resentment, jadedness, regret, or just plain old assholery if I didn't reckon with my ideas and expectations about being an artist.

None of these feelings were helped by the recent implosion of my personal life. Six months before filing those unpayable taxes, my husband and I split up. I was emotionally devastated by the divorce. I was also, quite suddenly, broke. P and I had been galaxies from rich by Manhattan standards, but it became painfully clear after our split just how far my writing/adjuncting income was from the level required to sustain a life in New York.

Eventually I landed a part-time managing editor job with an academic journal. I tried to comfort myself with a mental list of famous writers who had had day jobs: T. S. Eliot the banker, Wallace Stevens the insurance lawyer, William Carlos Williams the doctor, Van Morrison the window cleaner, Kurt Vonnegut the car dealer, Mark Twain the steamboat pilot, Toni Morrison the book editor, Charlotte Brontë the governess, Virginia Woolf the publisher, Jack London the *oyster pirate*. Plus, my love affair with personal essays and narrative travel writing definitely didn't pay the bills.

Yet despite having no financial choice in the matter, I fretted about a Bartleby the Scrivener type descent into monotonous office life. Twenty hours a week would surely soon enough become twenty-five, thirty, forty . . . I had gotten further as a writer than I ever had with music, but at thirty-three I found myself again facing a gap between expectations and reality and wondering what it meant to endure as an artist.

Potential

We've reached the *Webster's* dictionary portion of this introduction. Here's a definition of potential: "existing in possibility: capable of development into actuality." *Webster's* also notes how we have turned it into a loaded word:

"Potential can be either good or bad. Studying hard increases the potential for success, but wet roads increase the potential for accidents. But when a person or thing 'has potential,' we always expect something good from it in the future." Despite it being a neutral term, in our culture, *potential* has become infused with *promise*.

After watching my Interlochen campmate in his latest film, I couldn't stop thinking about how spectacularly Ben had manifested his artistic potential at the exact moment I was questioning mine. It made me wonder: Where had our other camp friends ended up?

A few days after the movie, I pulled out an old photo album of us in all our tween glory. There was Lizzie, the lithe ballerina, hugging wild Tamar, the gorgeous actress. There was Jenna, the competition-winning violinist, and Sarah, flute in hand. There was Eli, a skater kid who drew elaborate comic books; my aloof crush Daniel, an actor; and sweet, gangly Adam, another theater kid. In one shot my actress/artist friend Dalia sat off to the side, her head turned away, staring out at the freezing lake. The photo was taken a few days before she got kicked out of camp. Finally, there was my childhood frenemy Michelle, the violist I was constantly measuring myself against. These people were the most talented kids I ever knew.

Those Interlochen summers were the most self-assured time of my life: before quitting viola in college set my identity adrift, before getting a book contract in my mid-twenties mistakenly left me expecting to become a full-time author, and before my marriage fell apart. Those were magical days before anyone had tasted real success or failure, before anxieties and self-doubt had settled in beside art. We were ambitious but not calculating, hopelessly earnest with no shortage of energy.

Had my campmates become artists or had they abandoned their early talents? Having left behind the relatively even playing field of our exploratory twenties, were they, like me, grappling with whether they had fulfilled their potential? Or had they achieved exactly what they wanted? Ben had made a career of doing exactly what he was already doing brilliantly at eleven, but what about the rest of us?

Let me pause here to acknowledge that pondering a question like *"Have I fulfilled my potential?"* is clearly a luxury. It's an inquiry psychologist Abraham Maslow would argue sits well above basic human necessities like food, water, and safety, as well as needing love, friendships, and self-esteem. At the very top of Maslow's hierarchy of needs is self-actualization: "to become more and more what one is, to become everything that one is capable of becoming." That's when we start asking ourselves questions like: Am I pursuing my passion? Am I happy? Am I married to my soul mate? The writer Rebecca Solnit would probably call these "Cadillac problems."

Yet here I am, struggling nonetheless. Maybe you are, too. If so, let's start this Cadillac's engine, roll down the windows, and begin our metaphoric journey together.

"*Methodology*"

This book revolves around eight of my former campmates. I am going to share with you what came up in my conversations with them about potential and creativity. I've also incorporated relevant research, personal experience, and quotes from artists, psychologists, historians, philosophers, scientists, even radio hosts. Radio hosts can be *very wise*.

Spoiler alert: None of the people profiled in this book are famous. So if you're after an interview with film star Ben Foster, you're barking up the wrong book, but allow me to point you in the direction of the internet. I want to acknowledge that my group of friends at Interlochen was mostly white and middle class. I am writing through the lens of my limited experience; still, I'm hopeful my journey will resonate with others. In these pages you'll find a creative class of adults who fall somewhere between Beethoven and street buskers, a divide that exists in every field but feels especially vast in creative ones. I chose to profile them because I'm not convinced outliers are where we should look for role models, or, at least, not the only place we should look.

That being said, I've included quotes from and anecdotes about famous artists like Virginia Woolf and Philip Glass because while writing this book I learned there is no monolithic artist, no singular model for balancing the creative with the practical. Also, when it comes right down to it, many of us share some common struggles no matter where we are in our careers.

There is also the small detail of some of my favorite advice coming from sources who are not exactly exemplars of mental health (like Woolf). But I've always subscribed to an *Alice in Wonderland* worldview in that regard: just because you give yourself very good advice doesn't mean you follow it. Besides, we all know wisdom doesn't come only from the light. It often comes from dark nights of the soul.

My thoroughly unscientific criteria for inclusion was subjective and intuitive. I asked myself: *Is this something that helped me grapple with ideas about creativity and potential? Is it something that helped me navigate being an adult?* I pulled in anything that felt like a North Star guiding me on this journey. I hope some of my North Stars will also be yours, but of course there is no one-size-fits-all solution to navigating the distance so many of us feel between what we want and what we've got.

This is my story of being a former musician who never fully made peace with quitting and a current writer unsure of what her future holds. It is a book for anyone who has given up a childhood dream and grappled with that loss or with late-night what-ifs, for anyone who has aspired to do what she loves for a living and had doubts along the way, and for those of us somewhere in between emerging and established in our careers. It is also a love letter to the artistic life in its various forms. It celebrates our infinite creative potential as adults in all its beautifully complex and imperfect glory.

I admit I hoped by tracking down my old friends I could sprinkle a little fairy dust from those heady childhood summers on my adult life. Maybe I could even find my way back to the starry-eyed girl I used to be, so sure of exactly who she was going to be when she grew up.

2

I Was Going to Be
an Art Monster Instead

Jenna stood on a podium in front of her high school orchestra students. At thirty-two, she uncannily resembled my childhood friend. She was still a petite five-two with the same blunt bangs. Her thick brown hair was tucked back in a jaunty ponytail, while the teenage girls in the room wore their locks long and free. She held a conductor's baton in her right hand. An open violin case sat open off to one side, her instrument peeking out, the bow that had once belonged to her grandfather rosined and ready.

The wall behind Jenna was decorated with laminated prints of famous composers, the type that had adorned my childhood music room: Béla Bartók with receding silver tresses and a stern expression; Beethoven scrutinizing an orchestral score; Georges Bizet depicted as middle school history teacher meets bearded Brooklyn hipster.

"Interlochen made me who I am," Jenna was telling her students. She invoked the camp often to them. "That's a pretty big deal, guys."

They nodded politely, some starry-eyed at the idea of

this formative setting, others skeptical that their teacher had ever *really* been a teenager.

Jenna told her students we were best friends at camp but hadn't seen each other since we were their age. She said I was a writer doing a kind of "where are they now?" project about the kids we went to Interlochen with and that I had flown to Chicago all the way from New York City to reunite. This was all true, but I hadn't yet conveyed to Jenna how full of personal and professional doubts I was lately. I thought I should at least buy her dinner before dumping my existential crisis on her.

Maybe to hold her students' waning attention, Jenna confessed that at camp we both had a crush on the same shy cellist.

"Yeah, but unfortunately he didn't know we existed," I said. A few of the girls tittered.

"We google-stalked him last night," Jenna said. "He's still a cellist."

The girls who had laughed now looked mortified that their respectable conductor would stoop to such childish antics.

"Because you're playing music," Jenna continued, "every single person in here will most likely have that as part of your life forever. No matter what you end up doing."

JENNA HERSELF couldn't remember a time before music. She started on the violin at three years old, the same age Itzhak Perlman began teaching himself to play using a toy fiddle and Yo-Yo Ma was goofing around on the violin and viola before finally getting serious at age four with the cello.

"My mom said I had a good ear," Jenna had told me over the phone. "I picked things up quickly. There was a trial lesson, and I guess I nailed it, at three. I was lucky that I loved and excelled at what my parents wanted for me."

In a fun twist of familial fate, Jenna's parents actually met in a community orchestra that rehearsed in the very room where she now taught. Her dad, who himself had gone to Interlochen as a teen, was an excellent clarinet player, and her mom rocked a mean double bass. What luck indeed that Jenna's passion so neatly aligned with that of her musical parents. She never had to be bribed or cajoled to practice. She also never had to prove music was a worthy and achievable career path to parents who might see it as merely a hobby.

Her first concert as a kid was at Orchestra Hall, where the Chicago Symphony performs. A pint-size Jenna played only two songs, but she remembers that her entire family came and made a big deal of the concert. Backstage they presented her with a big bouquet of roses.

Her middle school didn't have an orchestra, but that's when Jenna started going to Interlochen. She spent six summers at camp.

"At home, I was just this odd duck who played an instrument. '*Oh, there's the girl who does violin. What's that about?*'" she said. But at Interlochen she fit right in.

When she was eleven, Jenna won the Concerto Competition, Interlochen's highest musical honor. I wasn't there that summer, but I can picture her standing center stage in her concert attire uniform: red sweater, navy socks, corduroy knickers chosen a century earlier supposedly to protect the modesty of lady cellists. Her navy knee socks would have marked her status as a Junior Girl. The entire camp, two-thousand-plus kids, would have been in attendance to watch her perform the first movement of Vivaldi's Concerto in A Minor, a piece favored by precocious young violinists (or their teachers), full of impressive runs and trills.

It was at Interlochen that Jenna had what she called an epiphany about the direction of her adult life. She was sixteen. "We were playing Mozart's *Jupiter* Symphony. I was sweating; it felt like a hundred degrees. And I just had a moment. Music is it. It's been here this whole time."

After high school she studied close to home at Northwestern, one of the country's top music schools. Family had always been really important, and she had no desire to live away from her parents and sister. During her freshman year of college, Jenna decided to major in music education instead of performance. She wanted to be a musician, but she also wanted to go to parties and spend lazy mornings with her vegan non-musician friends in their eccentric co-op. Those were the kinds of things you couldn't do if you were practicing all the time.

Her parents had early on planted the seed that teaching would be a stable, secure version of a musician's life. They knew Jenna had significant talent, but they also knew it was nearly impossible to make it as a soloist or even to get through the many rounds of auditions for a spot in an orchestra (or make it through with self-esteem intact). And while she'd loved playing in rock and folk bands in high school and college, being in a band professionally would mean traveling all the time. She didn't think she could have a family that way, and she wanted one. So just as her love of the violin had aligned with her parents' love of music, becoming a music teacher was also an easy decision for her.

Her Northwestern instructor wasn't happy about her choice but offered to still take her on as a student even though he typically worked only with performance majors. That he would make this exception is a testament to Jenna's talent. I bet he hoped she'd change her mind.

It wasn't that Jenna wasn't ambitious. She'd beat out more than a hundred qualified applicants for her current job at a top school in the most diverse district in Illinois. Her orchestras had incredible reputations in the area. But given her teacher's feedback that she was good enough to be a performer, I couldn't quite believe she hadn't been tempted to choose that path, like I had been as a kid.

Real Artists Are Art Monsters

When I visited Jenna in Chicago, the impression I got of her life was that it was a balanced artistic one. Her job as a music teacher fed her creative side while also giving her summers and other school breaks off to spend with her husband and baby. If I hadn't known her as a kid, this would have struck me as perfectly lovely. But I'd witnessed her abundant early talent, and caught up as I was in conflicted feelings about my own potential, I couldn't help but feel like she kind of, well, *owed* her talent an attempt to be the absolute best on the biggest possible stage.

And it seemed to me that people who strove for that kind of greatness weren't well-rounded spouses and parents and high school orchestra conductors. They were art monsters. I stole that phrase from Jenny Offill's brilliant novel *Dept. of Speculation*, about a woman considering what it means to be an artist once you become a spouse and mother. In it, the unnamed narrator tells us she had planned to be an art monster instead of getting married: "... art monsters only concern themselves with art, never mundane things. Nabokov didn't even fold his umbrella. Véra licked his stamps for him."

I believed that *real* artists are art monsters. They choose art above all else. They are workaholics like Leonard Cohen, who once admitted in an interview: "I'm actively working on songs all the time. Which is why my personal life has collapsed. Mostly I'm working on songs." They are brilliant, of course, but make terrible spouses and parents because they care more about art than anything else: think Bukowski and Beckett and Lord Byron and Dickens and Kafka and Roth and Hemingway and Faulkner and Spark and West and Sexton and George Sand.

The art monster trope is also intimately tied up with the suffering, self-destructive artist stereotype. The kind of imbalance great art requires is often connected with mental illness and addiction. Some artists perpetuate the idea that their pain is the source of their work. "My fear of life is necessary to me, as is my illness," wrote the artist Edvard Munch, who possibly had bipolar disorder. "Without anxiety and illness, I am a ship without a rudder. . . . My sufferings are part of my self and my art. They are indistinguishable from me, and their destruction would destroy my art." While others, like Van Gogh, famous for that whole cutting-off-his-ear incident, worried about how mental illness would hinder instead of help their creativity.

Regardless of how great artists see themselves, our culture romanticizes artistic suffering. We aspire toward balance while we are simultaneously captivated by stories of reclusive writers, eccentric entrepreneurs, and beautiful mind mathematicians. Any tortured genius will do, really.

The idea of the tortured artist is a product of the Romantic era, when the romanticized idea of madness itself took hold. Art was where "unbalanced views should be kept, as far away from religion and politics as possible." Fast-forward to clickbait lists like "Famous Geniuses with Weird Habits" and "10 Brilliant Writers Who Were Mentally Disturbed"—and if you're anything like me, you feel a weird mix of appalled and intrigued when you read them. I suppose it's understandable these lists garner more traffic than one called, say, "9 Artists Who Are Also Happy Moms" or "10 Writers Who Aren't on Antidepressants." There is no consensus among those who study mental illness and creativity regarding the exact nature, if any, of the link. Nevertheless, the link persists.

Even though it sounds like a nightmare to be (or to be

AND THEN WE GREW UP | 30

in a relationship with) most of these examples, I find it tempting to think that greatness requires an eccentric mind, or at least cultivating eccentric habits out of step with the behavior of ordinary folks in order to unleash your full potential. For example, I have a particularly ridiculous penchant for thinking that if I could just embrace a poly-phasic sleep schedule like Thomas Edison, Leonardo da Vinci, or Salvador Dalí (who apparently nodded off holding a key so that it would wake him up when it dropped), then boy oh boy, I could *really* get some work done. Even if I could just wake up at four A.M. like Haruki Murakami or five A.M. like Toni Morrison, I'd be better able to tap into my talent. Although, James Joyce woke up at ten A.M. and still did very well, I tell myself when I sleep in on the weekends.

I believed from an early age that to pursue an artistic passion meant I needed to be dedicated as exclusively as possible to it—potentially sacrificing happiness, family, even sanity. I believed what the writer Susan Sontag said: "There is a great deal that either has to be given up or be taken away from you if you are going to succeed in writing a body of work."

Art monsters definitely didn't become teachers instead of performers, as Jenna had. And they'd rather starve than take day jobs, as I recently had. They followed passion, not paychecks. This is art monster mythology sprinkled with a dash of American dream "do what you love" cultural mes-saging, of course.

There is a hidden challenge in this art monster mythology. If you can be happy doing something else, if you would survive untortured not Making Art, not sacrificing everything to the muse, then you weren't really an artist in the first place. This mythology also glamorizes mental health issues, addiction, and a wide variety of bad behavior, and it turns artists into mythical creatures when in reality they are, as the comedian Hannah Gadsby puts it, "very much of this world." I knew all this. And yet I admit it *hooked* me, this idea that the single-mindedness required to be an artist stood in opposition to Jenna's balanced approach to her artistic, work, and family life. She was no art monster, not even close.

THE NIGHT after watching Jenna conduct, I went to see her folk-rock band. Let's call them The Whales. The brick-walled Elbo Room where they were performing had the feel of a cozy half-finished basement. Bare lightbulbs drooped from the ceiling. Dusty bottles lined a long, cracked mirror behind the bar. The beat-up leather stools were full of Jenna's friends and fans.

Jenna didn't just play kick-ass fiddle. She also rounded out the group's three-part harmonies. At Interlochen, Jenna had auditioned for the chorus with an enthusiastic Lisa Loeb cover, but she didn't make the cut. For years, she wondered if she had a terrible voice, but now her alto was a confident, bluesy twang.

"I can hear the harmonies," she told me over drinks after her show.

The Whales had a decent following in Chicago, though Jenna was quick to tell me they weren't trying to make it.

"We're just having fun," she said.

Two years earlier, after a divorce, off-loading her house in a short sale, and moving into a dilapidated downtown walk-up previously inhabited by two chain-smoking painters, Jenna decided that what would make her most happy in the aftermath of her breakup was to be in a band like she had been in back in high school. Craigslist led her to The Whales. And The Whales led her to Kent, the group's lead singer, now her husband.

When she showed up to audition, Kent asked if she could improvise.

"What key?" she said. She tucked her instrument under her chin.

"F," Kent said. He rolled up one plaid sleeve and started to play a honky-tonk Webb Pierce song about being tired of waiting for a girl to come around and finally notice him.

After the second chorus, Kent nodded to Jenna and watched as she blew the barn doors off the apartment with her fiddling, scaling the neck of her instrument like Everest.

"She was just so incredibly good," Kent told me.

That afternoon Kent fell for Jenna's violin playing, and before too long he fell in love with Jenna, too. Cut to marriage, a baby, a pending offer on a house in the suburbs, a night or two a month rocking out onstage together, and days spent sharing her love of music with high school kids.

I know it's silly to think that being an artist requires being an art monster, that if you're serious about it, you can't make room for babies and husbands and day jobs because it is an all-or-nothing endeavor. But it was a story I'd been telling myself for a long time, even using it to help explain why my marriage had fallen apart. My ex and I fought constantly over how much time I spent writing: for me, never enough, and for him, far too much. The more I pulled away and into my work, the harder he tugged me closer. (I don't recommend this particular relationship dynamic, if you happen to be shopping around for one.)

The trope of the selfish artist in part probably originates in the premise that to develop an artistic skill (or plenty of other skills), you must spend a lot of time alone practicing it. And people who have a high tolerance for this kind of focused solitude are both admired and judged by our simultaneously workaholic and balance-obsessed culture. But for every example of a tortured loner artist, there is someone who has integrated work and love. Take Véra. She didn't just lick Vladimir's stamps. She was his "first reader, his agent, his typist, his archivist, his translator, his dresser, his money manager, his mouthpiece, his muse, his teaching assistant, his driver, his bodyguard (she carried a pistol in her handbag), the mother of his child, and, after he died, the implacable guardian of his legacy."

I knew art didn't happen in isolation. All I'd had to do was read the acknowledgments section of any book I loved to have that point hammered home, even if the only name we usually remember is the author's. In an attempt to cure my art monster addiction with science, I even found a study in which after interviewing a variety of successful artists and scientists, researchers concluded that the majority of them "need support from significant others, especially during creative breakthroughs . . . emotional support, unconditional acceptance, a sense of security, and a sense of belonging."

And there are countless examples of creative partnerships like Vladimir and Véra (many of them made possible thanks to your sponsor Gender Inequality, but that's a whole other chapter of a whole different book): Salvador Dalí had Gala, Virginia Woolf had Leonard, Frida Kahlo had Diego, Raymond Carver had Tess, Joan Didion had John, Alfred Stieglitz had Georgia, Percy Bysshe Shelley had Mary, Truman Capote had Jack, Simone de Beauvoir had Jean-Paul. Today there are writer couple goals like Dave Eggers and Vendela Vida, Ayelet Waldman and Michael Chabon, and Zadie Smith and Nick Laird, just to name a few of my favorite literary power couples.

Jenna and Kent had an artnership, too. They were both musicians. They practiced and performed together in a band, often playing and singing together at home. Jenna had integrated her personal and professional lives remarkably well, but she also had an artistic partner, which maybe made that easier. For me, the two spheres had always been distinct from each other. I *wanted* them to be integrated, but I didn't know how to pull that off. And if I struggled so much with balance in relationships, how would I ever throw kids into the mix, as Jenna had done, having chubby-cheeked Ellie a year after marrying Kent? Art monsters definitely weren't moms, at least not ones whose kids didn't end up with hefty therapist bills. You have no choice but to adjust your ambitions somewhat if you want to balance your various identities: teacher, parent, spouse, musician, and so forth. Jenna understood this and didn't see it as a cost—she saw it as necessary compromise—but I wasn't so sure.

And forget the high stakes of relationships and babies for a moment. I was wary of anything that ate into my writing time. More and more of adult life these days seemed to be taken up with, well, adulting. Just those basic boring tasks that eat up huge chunks of time: cooking, commuting, cleaning, folding, grocery shopping, financial planning, insurance getting, apartment hunting. Ad infinitum.

Many tedious grown-up tasks were so infuriating not only because they took up time when you'd rather be doing other things but because they were on an *endless loop*. It didn't matter if you lost twenty minutes yesterday doing the dishes; you would have to wash them again today, tomorrow, and the next day. Unless a rich aunt died and left you her fortune, you were gonna do those dishes for the rest of your mortal life.

Art monsters didn't care about dishes. They didn't care about picking up the dry cleaning. They cared only about—you guessed it—*art*. But when I spent time with Jenna at her house with her baby and Kent, I didn't see her resisting or resenting these mundane tasks of domestic life. There were times she was overwhelmed, she told me. There were days it felt like she was spread too thin. But on the whole she was thriving in a balanced space she had created that encompassed both the creative and the practical.

And anyway, what if I did sacrifice it all to the muse, if I doubled down on the idea that having a partner or kids or steady paycheck or consistently clean dishes would spell the end of my artistic ambitions? Then what? I had now been on this earth long enough to realize that if I was to sacrifice other parts of my life to writing, it guaranteed nothing other than the sacrifice. "In the long run we are all dead, and none of us is Proust," as Anne Enright summed it up. And if someone who won the Man Booker Prize feels that way, what hope do the rest of us have?

The Balanced Conductor

All of these questions were whizzing around in my neurotic brain the breezy May day I met Jenna at her school. She gripped a thin white baton and raised it to chest height, a signal to her students to get ready.

"One and two and three and four and . . ."

On her downbeat the first-chair cellist, a wiry girl in strappy Roman sandals, began her solo. She started out forte, then grew incrementally softer. She was excellent, perfectly in tune and able to capture the mournful elegance of Fauré's *Élégie*, written by the heavyhearted composer at thirty-four after a broken engagement. Although Fauré at that point was more our age than hers, she had that knack of precocious young musicians to express emotions well beyond their years.

Despite the cellist's best efforts, the piece began to

unravel after ten or so bars. When the first-chair flautist entered, she sounded shaky. Then the violas came in late. I took their mistake a little too personally for someone who had barely practiced in over a decade. *Come on, guys. This is why there are all those stupid jokes about us.* How is lightning like a violist's fingers? Neither one strikes in the same place twice. How do you get a viola section to shut up? Write "solo" on all their parts.

"Okay, let's stop right there," Jenna said. "Not bad, not bad. Violas, try to get ready a bit earlier, otherwise it's like"—she gasped and put her hand to her heart—"'It's time!' You should be ready earliest of anyone because they should be following you. So here's the deal. I'm listening to Zoe." She turned toward the cellist. "I'm following her, and she has the freedom to take a little more time. So you cannot be on autopilot, and I felt like you are a little bit. You need to follow me, and I'm following her."

She redirected her attention to the flautist in need of a boost in confidence. "Carly, I think your sound is coming out really beautifully for that first solo. All right, one more time. The opening."

I heard the slight adjustments the students made when they started over, as well as where they were trying to adjust but couldn't quite manage it, that frustrating gap between desire and ability.

Jenna let her students venture a minute more into the piece this time until the horns royally screwed the symphonic pooch.

"Horns," Jenna said, "you're a little bit late. Can I hear that again, please? If you practice nothing between now and the concert, except for those six notes, I'd be okay with that. Well, probably not, but you get my point. Those notes need to be so pure and true. And one and two . . ."

After they played, she lowered her baton.

"Well, that was the best time so far. Now let me hear the oboe alone. Listen to the beauty of this, everyone."

Jenna closed her eyes. The oboist's chest rose and fell as she played. She was really good, just like the cellist. I wondered if they planned to pursue music professionally. I found myself hoping the answer was yes, then immediately talking back to myself to ask why on earth I would wish them that kind of potential frustration and disappointment.

Jenna gestured for the rest of the orchestra to join in. "Remember, cellos, you're really expressive, vibrato. Okay, Lucy, you can play out a little bit more. Even though it says piano, especially since you're doubling the clarinet part. *Dah de dah dah dah dah.* Great! You got it."

The forty-five minutes proceeded like this, Jenna stopping and starting, balancing sincere praise with diplomatic critique, talking them through the piece section by section, urging them to connect with the music, singing bars every now and then to drive home her point. She was utterly confident with that baton, the way a conductor must be, strategically coaxing better and better playing from her musicians.

"That was it, violins!" she said. "You did it. Good job. Let's give them some orchestra applause." The students snapped their fingers like beatniks at a poetry reading. Then the bell rang and they scrambled off to their next class.

After the room had emptied out, we leafed through Jenna's camp photo album and relived our old crushes and competitors. Jenna remembered exactly who had kissed whom at the Date Gate, where boys and girls parted ways after a concert date, the only camp-sanctioned form of courting. We talked about our ancient camp conductor, Mr. Suttle, so thin and unsteady on the podium that we were continually shocked he was still standing after a three-hour rehearsal. At least once a week he leveled his favorite adage at a camper caught racing in as the orchestra was tuning up: "To be on time is to be late; to be *early* is to be on time."

"It's surreal seeing you up there conducting," I said to the adult Jenna sitting next to me.

"I know!" she said. "Sometimes I hear myself talking to the students and suddenly I see myself sitting in the violin section when I was their age, and it feels like I was *just* there."

"I miss playing in an orchestra," I said.

"You still can! Join a community orchestra. I was part of one until I had the baby, and it was great."

A few months earlier, I'd actually reached out to a local orchestra to see if they needed violas. They did, as orchestras seemingly always do, but week after week I found excuses not to go. In my head, I still thought of myself as a violist. In reality, my skills had atrophied long ago. Yet I continued to torture myself with the expectation that any day now I'd start practicing again, unsure of why I couldn't just let it go already and move on.

Jenna had told her students they would always have music in their lives, but I was stuck in some lapsed musician's Dante's circle of failed-potential hell. I missed playing—I *wanted* to play—but every time I picked up my viola, every time I even heard a classical piece I used to play, Telemann's Concerto in G Major, a Bach cello suite, Barber's *Adagio for Strings*, I experienced afresh the first great disappointment of my adult life. This visceral response was hooked into my art monster all-or-nothing thinking, too. The idea of playing as a hobby seemed impossible when I had once been a Serious Musician.

"I'm so rusty," I said. "It's depressing."

"That's hard for me, too," she said. "It's hard to pick up pieces I played in college. I'm like, 'How the hell did I do that? Those runs.' I'll think back to junior high and think: *Man, I was really good. At twelve. What happened?*"

It was obvious that we had very different definitions of *rusty*. Jenna had plucked her violin out of its case several times during the orchestra rehearsal to demonstrate passages for her students. Her playing was just as exceptional as I remembered it, but then, even when we were kids she had worn her immense talent lightly, whereas somewhere along the way I had gotten my ego all twisted up in mine.

For me, talent was everything. Well, talent coupled with art monster ambition.

When I asked Jenna what advice she gave students who wanted to pursue music as a career, she had no idea I had loaded up the question with so much psychic baggage.

"For the ones who are really good, and that is a very small percentage, maybe 2 percent, I say to try," she said. "Otherwise, you'll always wonder what if. To everyone else I say: Use this experience to help you become better at whatever it is you decide to do. But it's difficult to know even with the exceptional ones if you should push. I have a kid right now—a senior, a violinist—and he's incredible. Both of his parents are professional violinists, and they say, 'We're worried we created a monster, because he's so set on pursuing music. That's all he wants.'"

"He's an art monster," I said.

"A *what*?" she said.

When I explained it to her, Jenna was far too grounded a person to traffic in any of my art monster mythology. "What you have to do to be an artist is produce art," she told me.

"But to produce *great* art, don't you have to devote yourself exclusively to it?" I asked.

Jenna wouldn't take the bait. "My concern is balance," she said. "It's especially hard for women. I have worked so hard to achieve the success and career I chose, but I also want to be fully present as a wife and mother. You want to do great in both. Kent stays at home with Ellie, and I'm very lucky that he's so supportive."

I'd always viewed balance as something one achieved on an individual level, but Jenna and Kent had a kind of intra-relationship balance. (Although, unlike Jen, Kent did at one point hope The Whales would make it big, so maybe he is the one I should have asked about whether he's happy with how things turned out.)

I had no idea how creative ambition and life balance could coexist, because achieving balance seemed to imply being content, and didn't contentment mean you were no longer "hungry"? And if you lost your hunger, didn't you one day wake up in the suburbs helicopter parenting a couple of kids or working at a soul-sucking corporate job? You stopped making art. You stopped being passionate. You stopped being *you*.

But Jenna has never stopped being herself. And she is totally happy with her music without being even the tiniest bit an art monster about it. In fact, she is so grounded it is almost suspect. Every few months after our visit, I'd call her to catch up and ask a few more questions, always working up to an unsubtle attempt to ferret out if she was really and truly as satisfied as she seems.

One time I asked what her definition of professional success was.

"I've always wanted to do well," she said cryptically.

During another conversation I asked if she'd ever gotten nervous performing, thinking maybe this was why she had decided not to pursue a career as a soloist.

"I did, definitely," she said. "In my teens I started to shake before my auditions. My knees would literally knock together." Aha! A pleasant smugness washed over me, but the feeling was fleeting. "But it only lasted a few months because I learned that if I really overprepared, I would play fine even if I was nervous, and then one day I just stopped being nervous."

"You never had *any* doubts?" I said.

"I really love what I do," she said. "But sometimes it can be tough to keep up with everything. There is so much paper work, planning, and politics that can cloud why I'm here. Once in a while I wonder, if I had pursued being a pediatrician, a career I briefly considered as a kid, what my life might have been like. But I know I made the right choice. Knowing I have even a small impact on the lives of my students is so rewarding. Every day is different, and I get to create art. That's amazing."

I finally came right out with it. "So you got exactly what you wanted?"

I knew despite my attempt to sound breezy that the question had a tinge of "those who can't do, teach" condescension. If she picked up on it, she didn't say anything.

"I don't know that I always knew exactly what I wanted. It's just that over the years my perspective has mellowed. Before I had a family, I would have said my dream would be touring with a band. But now it doesn't appeal to me in the same way. I mean, if Arcade Fire said, 'Let's go on tour, Jenna...'"

She went quiet. Was she imagining herself onstage in front of enough fans to fill a thousand Elbo Rooms?

"Would you go?" I said.

"Maybe I would. Maybe. But I don't pine for that. I'm really happy with my life. I like where I am right now. I love teaching high school students. They get so excited about music. What I'm doing right now is really fulfilling. Look, I've always been idealistic but realistic."

Figuring out the right mix of idealism and realism seemed key to contentment. I wondered what it would feel like simply to accept where I am in the present without obsessing over the future. Every time I accomplished a goal, I barely took the time to celebrate it before refocusing my attention on another one off somewhere in the hazy distance.

Then again, meeting up with Jenna was sort of like starting a spiritual quest by dining with the Dalai Lama. Balance seemed to come easily to her, maybe because her talent has always been so big that she never felt she had anything to prove. Or maybe she limited her ambitions early on by deciding to become a high school orchestra teacher instead of a symphony musician or soloist. Maybe being a mother and a wife doesn't get in her way because she is driven entirely by a love of music, instead of something more ego-based.

Jenna was living a balanced artistic life, and it was helpful to see that up close. I didn't think my version of balance would look exactly like Jenna's. To be honest, I didn't know what it would look like, but Jenna *knew* balance, and spending time with her was the first time I'd acknowledged to myself that I wanted to shift my all-or-nothing art monster thinking.

Jenna had an early and intuitive understanding of the contours of her own ambition, whereas my own ambition had been a more unwieldy driving force for as long as I could remember. "Stay hungry," we tell creative types, and I had. From what I could tell online, my camp friend Tamar had, too.

3

On "Making It"

Tamar was an actress. She'd had some early success, most notably in our mid-twenties when she played the sarcastic, funny best friend on a sitcom. I had channel-surfed across the show one day and immediately recognized her still-magnetic presence. Tamar's adolescent cool and raspy voice had transformed into full-blown sex appeal. I kept sporadic track of her after that. A few years later, she played a buff action hero in another short-lived TV show and posed for *Maxim* in requisite near nakedness. In our early thirties, she played a mom in a web series. She had great comedic timing, delivering some of the funniest lines.

But it was easy to search out online that Tamar hadn't worked in TV or film since then. I'll admit, as I sleuthed, I was grateful not to be an IMDb-able actor. Yes, I wanted to be published; yes, I wanted to be read. But the most famous writer in the world isn't as visible or recognizable as a recurring sitcom character, so we can go more quietly unpublished than an actor can in a dry spell.

Tamar was the first person from Interlochen I reached out to. When I told her I was tracking down our old friends, she seemed genuinely excited about getting together to re-live our camp days.

"Interlochen is what formed me," she had said over the phone. "I went for six summers and attended the Academy during the year for all four years." The Arts Academy is Interlochen's private boarding high school. Jewel went there. So did Norah Jones and Rufus Wainwright.

At twelve, Tamar had been confident and outgoing, while the rest of us were in our awkward duckling stage. One summer she wore her flaxen hair in tight little buns all over her head, and *god,* she looked cool. She even knew how to make knickers stylish: order them one size too big and leave the bottom buttons undone. Genius. In a uniform designed to extinguish individual style, Tamar's shone through. She was talented, pretty, and charistmatic—a trifecta of good fortune for an aspiring actress.

On the phone, she was the same bubbly Tamar I remembered, even when she casually mentioned that she hadn't had the greatest career luck lately. "If you come out here, you'll see more a working waitress than a working actress," she said.

I assured her I had spent plenty of years working on and off in restaurants and had the roster of bartender/musician exes to prove it. If I'd had the relevant statistics at my fingertips at the time, I might also have mentioned that, say, the median pay for actors is $17.49 per hour; and for full-time writers, it's $20,000 a year; or that out of two million arts graduates in the nation, only 10 percent earn their living primarily as artists.

"Yeah, it's not always glamorous, is it?" she said. "But we keep going because we love it and we're driven."

Tamar told me she had just started taking acting classes with a very old, very expensive instructor who had mentored a handful of famous thespians. I asked if I could observe a class when I visited.

"The teacher is very private, so I doubt it. But the rest of my life is an open book," she said.

Two weeks later, after I had booked my ticket to L.A., my phone buzzed with Tamar's name.

"Hey, Rachel," she texted. "I'm really sorry but we can't meet up after all."

"Why not?" I texted back.

"I told my managers that you're a journalist and they said it wasn't a good idea. They think you'll portray me as a pathetic, struggling actress. They can't see any upside for me."

"I totally get your concerns," I wrote. "But from where I'm standing you've had a lot of success. Every career has peaks and valleys."

"I just can't do it. These guys are responsible for my career. I can't go against their advice."

"Okay," I conceded. "No worries. But I've already got my ticket for L.A. I'm going to be out there seeing family, anyways. Can we meet off the record for a drink? As old friends." I hoped she could tell I was sincere.

"That sounds great," she texted.

That was the last time I heard from her. I tried to reach her three times before I left, including one last Hail Mary call from the airport, but she never responded.

On Touching It

In Chicago, I had mentioned to Jenna that Tamar had gone MIA. We were looking through old camp photos and paused on one of Tamar at the beach. She wore a bright blue bathing suit and a coy smile. Back arched and chest forward, she knew how to pose and perform even then. In the background, our preteen guy friends pretended not to stare.

"It must be really hard to 'touch it' and then it seems like it stops," Jenna had said. "She went to the Academy, so it's different even from the intensity of our summers. She made a decision very early, and from what I see on Facebook, it must be very difficult where her career is now."

Thirty-three-year-old Tamar's Facebook feed was full of selfies. There she was posing with a mimosa in a silky black romper gazing out at the Hollywood Hills, hair slicked back in a bun. I scrolled down and found her pouty-lipped in a tight dress and stilettos. Sometimes the pic captured only fragmented body parts: two tan legs attached to a pink bikini bottom, thick blond brows paired with Pacific-blue eyes. Her Facebook followers were thoroughly engaged, doling out likes and compliments: "So so pretty!" and "Such a cutie!" and the oddly formal "Thank you for being so stunning."

I could tell from her page whenever pilot season rolled around because new headshots popped up with announcements about upcoming auditions. Some days she was effusive, but other days she wrote openly about how tough it was trying to make it in Hollywood. She made quips about the waitress/actor's life and posted accompanying pics in her diner uniform. Looking at her Facebook page felt like sneaking a read of someone's private diary, yet I couldn't tear myself away.

It reminded me of something I'd recently read in Ruth Whippman's *America the Anxious: How Our Pursuit of Happiness Is Creating a Nation of Nervous Wrecks*:

> This is social media's basic Faustian pact: you believe my Facebook fiction (and allow it to make you slightly envious and insecure), and I'll do the same for yours.
>
> Happiness is the currency of social media . . . Somehow, without ever discussing it, we have almost universally decreed social media to be a kind of personal PR agency, a forum for us to assemble a set of glittering promotional materials for our own lives.

Tamar was bravely breaking this Faustian pact of curated perfection. Yes, artists are supposed to suffer, but struggle is supposed to be a stop on the way to success. It's palatable as something you're referring to in the past, or as a colorful, inspiring anecdote in a larger narrative of success. But to be so candid about sometimes struggling, well . . . "Everybody loves the underdog," sings Ani DiFranco, "but no one wants to be him." This despite the fact that there are way more underdogs than breakout stars, thousands of Tamars for every Ben Foster.

Social media has made the experience of "touching it" more public than ever before. We shout our achievements from the digital rooftops, then hope no one notices our radio silence during periods there's nothing to shout about. A dry spell can feel dire instead of part of the natural ebb and flow of life because we're constantly scrolling through other people's greatest hits: promotions, awards, weddings, and completed marathons, in addition to everyday experiences like a good meal, a pretty sunset, or a walk in the park, cropped and filtered, and the emotional stakes are heightened by #gratitude and #goodtimes hashtags.

Tamar wasn't by any stretch a failure as an actor, but she also hadn't "made it," either. Well, depending on your definition of making it, of course. Sure, there are some broad metrics: money, power, prizes, fame—though in exactly what form and combination is an individual calculation. Then there is the definition I was raised to embrace: "making it" is doing what you love. As in: doing what you love *for a living.*

In *Originals: How Non-Conformists Move the World*, the psychologist Adam Grant counters the idea of ditching your day job to do what you love for a living by offering up examples of those who succeeded while hedging their bets. The founders of eyeglasses-by-mail company Warby Parker had day jobs when they started their business. So did Henry Ford; he was a chief engineer for Thomas Edison. The writer Stephen King kept various side gigs, including gas station attendant, for seven years after writing his first story, finally quitting after his first novel, *Carrie*, was published. As Grant explains it:

> Common sense suggests that creative accomplishments can't flourish without big windows of time and energy, and companies can't thrive without intensive effort. Those assumptions overlook the central benefit of a balanced risk portfolio: Having a sense of security in one realm gives us the freedom to be original in another. By covering our bases financially, we escape the pressure to publish half-baked books, sell shoddy art, or launch untested business.

Author Elizabeth Gilbert seems to agree with Grant. She tells us in *Big Magic: Creative Living Beyond Fear* that if she hadn't become a bestselling author she'd still be working part-time day jobs to make ends meet and wouldn't feel disappointed in the least. After all, she writes, she took "vows" to her art—she is fully committed to it—and that is enough. Her writing doesn't owe her anything in return.

And then there are those legendary artists who have had day jobs for decades, such as the composer Philip Glass, who once worked as a plumber and taxi driver. I thought often about an encounter Glass described with an art critic: "While working, I suddenly heard a noise and looked up to find Robert Hughes, the art critic of *Time* magazine, staring at me in disbelief. 'But you're Philip Glass! What are you doing here?' It was obvious that I was installing his dishwasher and I told him I would soon be finished. 'But you are an artist,' he protested. I explained that I was an artist but that I was sometimes a plumber as well and that he should go away and let me finish." My takeaway from this tale was that Glass wasn't precious about his identity as an artist, even if Hughes was. Glass was passionate but practical. He didn't think an artist couldn't also be a plumber.

But look. *Eat Pray Love*'s Elizabeth Gilbert *did* become successful enough to quit her day jobs, so we'll never really know how she would have felt if she'd become a fifty-year-old bartender who never earned her living solely from writing. Philip Glass gave up taxis and plumbing in his early forties. Adam Grant's ideas about balancing work and passion have turned him into a *New York Times* bestselling outlier who gives inspirational graduation speeches around the country. Also, Henry Ford became an automotive giant, Stephen King became a legendary horror writer, and the founders of Warby Parker became the guys with a gigantic flagship store in SoHo where every hip millennial goes for glasses.

Gilbert took vows to her writing? Well, I took vows, too, first to music and later to writing. I'm sure Tamar had pledged heart and soul to acting. (Probably at Interlochen!) And yet Tamar was waitressing, that age-old flexible-hours side gig for creatives. I was a managing editor half the week. One has to pay the bills, of course, and artists are kind of expected to have a backup plan because it's so common to fail at earning a living in the arts, but I couldn't help but think the benchmark of true success was the moment we could quit those day jobs for good.

We definitely weren't supposed to have to return to our day jobs after a period when we were successful enough to leave them behind. Remember that scene in *Friends* when Joey laments having to serve coffee at Central Perk? "I was an actor. Now I'm a waiter," he says. "It's supposed to go in the other direction." A more recent real-world example was when a photo went viral of *Cosby Show* actor Geoffrey Owens working at a Trader Joe's. We're collectively incredulous at these kinds of stories and I think it's because of this deep belief in linear success, in continually improving lives and careers, in "making it" as a final destination. But I knew plenty of writers, actors, and musicians who veered back and forth over time between artistic and non-artistic ways of making a living, myself included.

The psychotherapist Adam Phillips helps explain these expectations when he writes about how we are a culture "committed above all to science and progress—to create societies in which people can realize their potential, in which 'growth' and 'productivity' and 'opportunity' are the watchwords (it is essential to the myth of potential that scarcity is scarcely mentioned: and growth is always possible and expected)." We talk a lot about growth and potential but far less about the very common experience of "touching it"—whatever "it" is at any given moment before it slips away or morphs into some new elusive goal—then losing it, then maybe if you're lucky touching it again someday.

The Ambitious Screenwriter

An email from Adam, another camp friend, was waiting for me when my red-eye from Los Angeles touched down back in New York. I had just missed him on my trip to L.A., where he was a TV and film writer.

"What are you working on?" I asked during our first phone conversation.

"Well, my big headline is that a show I created is in its first season on MTV."

The show was about a teenage girl who had grown up in a Disneyland-type amusement park with a single mother whose job was playing a princess. The girl falls for a rich guy working there for the summer. High jinks ensue.

"It's trying to mine the Shakespearean world of class differences and kings and queens," Adam said. "With a weird MTV twist."

"Very cool," I said. "And how's it going?"

"We're waiting to see if it gets picked up for a second season. The critical reviews have been mixed, but more positive than negative. It got a very nice review in *EW* and *TV Guide*. *The New York Times* was a nice, fair review, but not glowing."

Adam's specialty as a writer in some ways stemmed from the time we knew each other. He was really good at re-creating the intensely felt emotions of adolescents so many of us dismiss as melodrama once we're older.

"I remember one time I put in a script about a teenage

girl a list called 'Things About Me That Suck,' and when people read it, they were like, 'That feels real.' And I'm like, 'Yeah, that's what girls wrote when they were fourteen.' My new show is pitched to teenage girls, too. That's not necessarily where I saw myself as a writer, but I feel like I'm really good at recalling emotions I've had or someone else has had and turning them into something that feels authentic."

Being attuned to teenage girls also comes from years of trying to decode what he used to think of as mysterious and powerful beings. His memories of our camp friends included the concrete details of an observant late bloomer: "Tamar had a very developed sense of herself. Jenna once gave me a really amazing hug." He also remembered Dalia, the friend I still couldn't find online despite my deep googling.

"I was totally in love with Dalia," he said. "She used to say, 'God, I need a cigarette so badly.' She was really dark. She once showed me a poem she had written that ended: 'If I blow my brains out on the floor, my mom will think: what a beautiful picture.'"

I told Adam about Tamar's disappearing on me, thinking he might have some insight into their shared world.

He sighed. "She's in a tough spot. Hollywood is horrible and ageist. For female actors, it only gets harder. The actress who plays the mom on my show is thirty-seven and looks twenty-two. It's a tough, tough business. If I wasn't coming off a period of good work . . ." He trailed off, but the implication was *we wouldn't be having this conversation.*

"Have you had enough success at this point that you believe in your own talent despite how tough it is?"

"The idea of talent is something I grapple with on a daily basis. Am I going up or down? Am I as good as I was yesterday? Will I be tomorrow? What's my trajectory? I am proud of my show, but in no way do I just breathe a sigh of relief."

"Do you think it's possible to relax—to just trust yourself so fully that you don't worry about what happens to your work?" I asked Adam.

As a response, Adam told me how one of his best friends from Interlochen is now a famous singer. "He is legit famous," Adam said. "Even he's not immune from these concerns. There's not anybody who is successful who doesn't worry that success will go away."

"What keeps you going?" I said.

"I started writing and directing plays in high school. Being able to take something that starts in your brain and then it becomes tangible and you get to share it with others— you bring it to life—that was a really exciting rush for me. I wanted to spend my life chasing it. People liked my first play. It got a really good response. But then I didn't get into the same writing program at my high school the following year and I was like, 'Did I peak at fifteen?'"

In college a film he wrote was the top short of his sophomore class, but then his junior-year film wasn't as good; it had a lot of technical problems. His senior-year film won a bunch of awards.

"And finally," Adam said, "I was like, 'Okay, it wasn't a onetime fluke, but also there are peaks and valleys.'"

"And you were okay with peaks and valleys?" I said.

"After that, I spent years shooting wedding videos and

trying to write a decent screenplay and I did worry. But by then I had realized this comes with the territory. Eventually I worked again. The projects piled up."

"Was there ever a moment when you thought, *This is it. This is my big break?*"

"I went out to L.A. with my former writing partner and we had a bunch of meetings based on a spec script. One producer liked the script and said she'd like to be in business with us on it. We walked out of that room and erupted in celebration as though this was the best thing that could have ever happened. Then we called our manager and he was like, 'Oh, cool, so what are you doing?' And we were like, 'This idea, this TV idea with this producer!' And he was like, 'Well, she's never done TV, but sure, it doesn't hurt to try it.'"

"What happened?" I asked.

"Nothing! We worked on it with her and we learned a lot, but it never got made. That moment of 'Oh, wow, this is my big break' is an expectation you have when you're younger. Of course we fantasize about that because people are presented to us all the time as having 'burst onto the scene from nowhere,' when that's really never the case. That's not how it has been with me or other people I know."

Adam's career, like Tamar's and mine, had ebbed and flowed. I had learned after my first book was published that creative success wasn't about one big break, but I still worried about slipping backward and somehow not being able to leap ahead again. So Adam's bluntly laying out the number of times he'd gone forward and back and forward again was helpful in thinking about my own trajectory. Enduring as a writer for Adam wasn't about a "making it" moment but about a constant process of trying and trying again. Something the photographer Tammy Rae Carland tells her art students has stuck with me as a useful reframing along these lines. She advises them to "view their careers as a checkerboard rather than a ladder."

"Do you think you're good at weathering the ups and downs?" I asked Adam.

"I think I'm okay with them, but I could be better. I weather it as well as the next guy. I think I have a basic faith in my work ethic at this point, and I know enough from having worked hard that mostly what I write at this point won't be shit. I write when I don't feel like working. I don't wait for the muse. And the dirty secret is the work on days I don't feel like it isn't necessarily any less inspired. I work five or six days a week, and seven if something is really pressing. I know some of those days will be all brainstorming. I'll realize I have nothing usable and that the only thing I learned is that I have nothing usable. But that's part of the process."

This American Life host Ira Glass once gave great advice for those starting out in creative fields to help them get to the point where they have this faith in their own work. Beginners can identify good work when they see it, he said, but don't yet have the ability to produce it. It can take years for your creative abilities to catch up with your creative aspirations. A lot of people get frustrated and quit during this time, but Glass says the key is to keep plugging away and churning out the work.

This is crucial encouragement for beginners, but if you endure long enough, you get used to this gap (however large or small it feels on any given day). But the kind of taking stock Adam was doing—"Am I going up or down? Am I as good as I was yesterday?"—often still lingers.

These are tricky questions because creative success is a thing other people bestow on you. And while success has a relationship to the quality of creative work, art is subjective. We all *know* this, and yet you still must think carefully about how much external validation you need, if any, to keep going, to weather the inevitable ups and downs of touching it. Are you determined to be Beyoncé famous, or are you happy in the middle of the pack? Are you happy doing the work even if it never gets published or produced?

On Ambition

Adam was coming to Manhattan soon, so we decided to continue our conversation in person. Unlike Jenna, the grown-up Adam barely resembled the kid version. He was still tall and slender, still a redhead, still funny, but he had grown out of his lankiness and into a much better haircut than the ear-length bob he used to sport.

When we met up for coffee at Grand Central Terminal, I asked Adam what he ultimately hoped to accomplish in his career. He rattled off a wide-ranging list: "I want to direct. I'd like to work in different mediums: theater, film. I love writing short stories. It would be great to rewrite some big sci-fi movie. I'd like to supervise other writers eventually; I like teaching as well."

I sat back in my chair and assessed him.

"What?" he said.

"I'm trying to figure out how you seem simultaneously so ambitious and so grounded."

"Look, I'm really ambitious," he said. "But I want to be a person first and an artist second. Also, I work in Hollywood, so I think the phrase *artist* is a loose one at best. Beyond that, the arts are inherently self-indulgent and about saying, 'Oh, I'm trying to express myself, so the world should give a shit.'"

I was reading the sculptor Anne Truitt's diaries at the time, and his words reminded me of something she wrote: "I refused, and still refuse, the inflated definition of artists as special people with special prerogatives and special excuses." It stuck in my mind because even though I never would have admitted it out loud, this was another belief I had unconsciously absorbed as part of the art monster mythology: the idea that artists are inherently special. They see and experience the world differently from nonartists; they are "more alive than the others," as the choreographer Martha Graham put it.

Adam, like Jenna, clearly didn't buy into these kinds of clichés about artists. He hadn't adjusted his ambitions in the same way as Jenna (he didn't have kids, a spouse, or a mortgage), but he had his own version of balance that kept him grounded: working hard without getting too caught up in his identity as an Artist.

But while not taking art too seriously seemed like part of Adam's strategy not to take himself too seriously, his belief that the arts were self-indulgent sounded suspiciously blasé for someone who clearly took writing very seriously and talked about his current and future projects with such enthusiasm.

"If the arts are really just self-indulgence," I asked Adam, "why not contribute something more meaningful to the world?"

"I was talking to my friend who works in education," he said. "I was saying that what he did was more important, and should I really be sitting around writing about my feelings? Did the world really need that? 'What if Jimi Hendrix had become a schoolteacher?' my friend said. 'Would that have been a better use of Jimi Hendrix's time? No, he's a great guitarist, so it's better that Hendrix provided the world with great guitar music.'"

"But Hendrix was *Hendrix*," I said. "We're talking about a level of talent that probably makes it easy not to ask yourself too many probing questions about your career path."

"Whether I'm talented or not is not really up for me to decide. I'd like to think I am. I hope I am. But mostly I believe in doing the work."

"Do you think there is a hierarchy of talent in the world?" I asked Adam. "Like, we each get a certain allotment and no more?"

"Yes," he said. "But it's not my job to worry about that, either."

I think a lot of ambition is, at its heart, about control. We convince ourselves that with enough ambition we can master money, success, clutter, time, parenting, mind-set—our entire world. And then our fantasy of our life will finally match its reality. (The flip side of ambition fueled by control is that whenever we fall short of our own expectations, we believe the fault is entirely ours. That we must simply *try harder*.) It was this element of control that Adam had removed from his own ambition. He wanted to achieve certain things, of course. He wanted success. But he did not believe that desire and hard work had a direct relationship to getting what he wanted. If I can put some scientist lingo in his mouth, he had made an important psychic distinction between correlation and causation.

Adam's ambition was tied to process instead of outcome. He had goals, not expectations. Yes, he took stock of his talent, but he didn't believe he had control over it, whereas I always had. I wanted to be more like Adam was—to be ambitious without being overly attached to the results of that ambition.

Like Adam, I believed in putting in the hours. I had practiced viola whether or not I felt like it. I put pen to paper or fingers to keyboard every day, even though what I wrote was sometimes so awful that when I read it twenty-four hours later I had to tell myself someone else had written it, possibly an intoxicated person with only a passing grasp of the English language.

But that was okay. That was the process. As Ann Patchett writes: "I can't write the book I want to write, but I can and will write the book I am capable of writing. Again and again throughout the course of my life I will forgive myself." I had learned to work mostly contentedly in that Ira Glass gap between what I envisioned for my work and what I produced because, like Adam, I loved doing the work. You have to in order to keep going.

We love the image of the writer/painter/musician startled awake by the muse at three A.M. She grabs the notebook by her bed and scribbles furiously, committing her inspired vision to paper before it flees her brain. She loses track of time, is impervious to thirst or hunger. Eventually she notices the sun has risen. She hears people walking to work below her window. And once in a while, this scenario *does* happen. But mostly the words do not burst forth in a feverish dream state, so you wake up when your alarm goes off and start writing anyway. Or you go to work and write at night, or on the weekends when the kids are napping, or for an hour a day at lunch.

I knew all this. I knew, as Dani Shapiro put it, that "the practice *is* the art." But . . . I *also* wanted to be read. *And* I wanted to make a living. *And* I wanted to have famous writer friends. And, and, and. I want, I want, I want.

I know, I know. An artist is supposed to be driven by passion, not by public validation. We're supposed to value intrinsic, not extrinsic, rewards. (The idea that you can't be serious about your art and also want to make money at it is yet another unhelpful myth about the artist.). But then one also needs to have ambition to progress, and what is ambition if not wanting? I'd been taught to value progress, just as I'd been taught to value passion, and I had no idea how to reconcile that conflict.

I felt a visceral resistance to what Adam had said about having no control over our own success or talent, because yes, I love to write, but I also apparently believe I am in fact owed something in return. I had signed some grandiose, meritocratic, imaginary contract with the universe regarding my potential. As long as I put in the hours, as long as my potential was fed by ambition and hard work, I would achieve whatever goal I set for myself—no matter how lofty or unlikely. Eventually I would be rewarded by morphing from a writer who was barely scraping by into a successful writer with no day job.

On Effort and Reward

Hard work (that is to say, putting in the hours) as a necessary component of success is a no-brainer kind of concept, but in the last few decades, an increasing number of researchers and journalists have focused on figuring out and explaining exactly how those at the top of their fields— from chess players to musicians to champion spellers and world-class memorizers—got there.

One of the most popular twenty-first-century formulas for achieving your potential is the "10,000-hour rule." "The idea that excellence at performing a complex task requires a critical minimum level of practice surfaces again and again in studies of expertise," writes Malcolm Gladwell in *The Outliers: The Story of Success.* "In fact, researchers have settled on what they believe is the magic number for true expertise: ten thousand hours."

Gladwell uses elite hockey players, the Beatles, Bill Joy, and Bill Gates as examples to argue it wasn't their talent that made the difference in their success. Instead, it was the ten thousand hours of hard work they put into honing their talents: "Practice isn't the thing you do once you're good. It's the thing you do that makes you good."

The science behind Gladwell's formula mostly belongs to K. Anders Ericsson, a Swedish psychology professor whose research on expertise has gone mainstream and who is often quoted in the news and interviewed on podcasts. In the early nineties, Ericsson and his colleagues proposed that individual differences in performance in music, sports, games, business, and other complex domains reflect accumulated amounts of deliberate practice. Ericsson isn't entirely on board with Gladwell's interpretation of his work. He has said Gladwell misinterprets the fact that ten thousand hours of practice is an average, not a tipping point. Some people need more practice and some less. He also takes issue with Gladwell's leaving out his core concept of deliberate practice. It's not merely how much you practice, Ericsson argues, but *how* you practice.

"How do I know if my one hour of practice is the same as your one hour of practice?" I asked Ericsson during a brief phone interview.

"Great question," he said. "If music teachers give the same assignment to students, then if they go off for a week and attain what was the goal of training, I would argue that is evidence that something changed. A domain where someone has accumulated knowledge of your performance—a stepladder of tasks of increasing performance. With deliberate practice, you have a goal where you weren't able to do something and then afterwards you are able to do it." Ericsson said that other than body height and size, he didn't know of any other genes necessary for someone to be successful in domains where those kinds of attributes don't matter.

The approved-by-science concept that practice is the great equalizer dovetails nicely with our American love affair with the idea that anyone can be or do anything she sets her mind to (except for physical feats like dunking a basketball or battling a 250-pound linebacker). But it didn't take much digging into the academic literature to find a slew of researchers who believe Ericsson has greatly oversimplified the relationship between talent, skill, and practice.

There's Ellen Winner, a Boston College psychology professor who studies prodigies. "I think Anders Ericsson has taken a provocative position that taken to an extreme cannot possibly be true," Winner told me. Nobody would deny that practice is necessary, but it's really hard to prove it's sufficient. "For instance, any child that's motivated to practice [for] huge amounts of time has to already have some innate ability in that skill driving him to practice. You cannot get a typical child to spend that time. If you're good at it, you can't tear yourself away. I call that the 'rage to master,' and it goes along with having high skill. But we have an egalitarian society, and that's why we don't like the idea of talent."

Brooke Macnamara, a psychology professor at Case Western Reserve University, told me that Ericsson's work relies on the premise that all people are the same and all tasks are the same. "But people and human performance [are] complex and individuals vary. We have all sorts of differences . . . Working memory capacities, central processing, intelligence. There are differences even in physical elements—different makeup of slow and fast twitch muscles, different max oxygen uptake. People don't want to talk about individual differences. It's very American to say anyone can do anything."

Macnamara mentioned a study of medical students in which each aspiring MD had eight hours of training on a specific task. If they passed, they moved on. If they failed, they received more training and took the test again. Those students who completed the task on the first try performed better at it than those who received more training and eventually passed. In other words, the ones who started out better remained better at the task even after their peers had more practice. She also told me about a study focused on pitch training for musicians. The amount of time it took for some students as opposed to others was measured in *years*.

"If I'm tone deaf," Macnamara said, "I'm going to have a much harder time. And I'll probably never get as far as someone who has perfect pitch."

There is evidence that what we learn (that is to say, what we practice) *does* change and shape the brain in certain ways, according to Macnamara. The area of the motor cortex responsible for the hands of violinists is more robust, for example. But this isn't the whole story. Macnamara implied that Ericsson had set up a sort of straw man in his research.

"One side says it's all training and practice," she said. "But nobody is on the other side. You have people who should be in the middle saying it's multiple factors, so that middle position now becomes the opposition."

Macnamara's work led me to the research of Zach Hambrick, a cognitive psychology professor at Michigan State University who directs the Expertise Lab. In the journal *Psychology of Learning and Motivation*, he and his coauthors argued that while deliberate practice appears to be an important piece of the expertise puzzle, it's only one piece, "and not necessarily even the largest piece."

What else matters? Relevant factors are age ("the evidence is consistent with the possibility that there is a critical period for acquiring some complex skills, just as there may be for language") and genetics (working memory capacity has been shown to be hugely important to musical prodigies, for example, and genes account for 50 percent of your abilities there). There's also "susceptibility to performance anxiety and to 'choking' under pressure or other personality-type factors that could impact performance directly, independent of deliberate practice."

Hambrick didn't hold back when we spoke on the phone:

"Ten thousand hours is not true. There is tremendous vari-
ability in becoming an expert."

Like Winner and Macnamara, he cited studies that had
received less media attention than Ericsson's but that offer
an alternate view of the expertise landscape. He told me
about a study of top chess players that found the number of
hours practiced varied wildly between 3,000 and 24,000,
and a study of swimmers that found levels of training were
less predictive at high levels. The national-level swimmers
had actually practiced *more* than the elite-level swimmers.

"We *have* to look at behavioral genetics—our genes influence the environment we create and select for ourselves,"
he told me. "There was an important discovery recently
that even practice turns out to be in part heritable. Think
about how differently inclined some people are to exercise
versus others. There is a study in Sweden looking at a twin
registry that found 40 to 50 percent variation across people
in practice is accounted for by genetic factors. This could
mean, for example, that those with high music aptitude are
more likely to practice and persist." (In other words, Ellen
Winner's "rage to master.")

Half an hour into our conversation, high on the complex
science of it all, I found myself rambling on to Hambrick
about my path with music. I told him about Interlochen,
about excelling in music as a kid, then hitting a wall with it
in college. I mentioned that I had speculated on and off
since I quit viola about the exact set of circumstances that
added up to my not being able to make it as a professional
musician.

Hambrick told me that as a teenager, he had been an excellent golfer. He wanted to play golf professionally, but then he went to college and realized as he looked around at the strongest players that he was nowhere near good enough. That's part of what led him to the science of expertise. (Ericsson has a similar origin story, but with chess.)

"So *maybe*," I said, "if we understood the nuanced science behind expertise we might not torture ourselves for thinking we never lived up to our potential."

"Well, um, maybe," Hambrick said politely. "What you're asking has scientific *and* philosophical dimensions, though. It's almost existential."

"It's *totally* existential," I said dreamily, probably making Hambrick consider whether he should have taken my call.

Another crucial piece of the puzzle, Hambrick emphasized, are opportunity factors. "Take your experience going to Interlochen, for example. Not everyone gets to go to Interlochen. It's on the nurture side of the equation. If we were to do a study and look at variations in people across experiences like that, I would wager a pint of beer what we would find is that this variable is also influenced by genetics. If you're pretty good at music, there's a good chance that your parents are pretty good at music. Their genes influenced the environment that you inherited from them. This included things like sending you to Interlochen versus a sports camp."

I thought of how Jenna had inherited her grandfather's bow, how her parents were both excellent amateur musicians who valued the arts. Opportunities are, of course, contingent on having the money to pursue them, yet one of America's must enduring ideologies is that no matter who you are, with enough hard work you can succeed. Take Adam. His parents had helped him pay his rent after college so that he could focus on writing. A decade later he still felt guilty about this advantage.

"They didn't pay for everything," he told me. "I did work a lot, but they helped me. I was someone whose parents helped fund my self-expression. That feels hard to justify. I know there are a lot of people who are really talented who had to work harder themselves to get these breaks."

Even at Interlochen, where we wore uniforms meant to dissolve class disparities, some kids paid full price and others were on scholarships. There were kids who would spend small fortunes at the Scholar Shop on sheet music and snacks and say, "Whatever, it's my parents' money." In contrast, there was a girl in my cabin one year who confessed that her parents "didn't eat out all year" so she could attend.

If there's a pop science concept that has taken over where the idea of ten thousand hours leaves off, it is psychology professor Angela Duckworth's notion of grit. In *Grit: The Power of Passion and Perseverance,* she writes: "[T]he highly successful had a kind of ferocious determination . . . First, these exemplars were unusually resilient and hardworking. Second, they knew in a very, very deep way what it was they wanted. They not only had determination, they had *direction.* It was this combination of passion and perseverance that made high achievers special. In a word, they had grit."

According to Duckworth, grit predicts success more reliably than talent or IQ and "anyone can learn to be gritty."

When we're told success is as simple as gritty perseverance or putting in ten thousand hours, it's a short walk to believing that failure must be all your own fault. Part of what nagged at me when I thought about the idea of my failed potential was having been given so many opportunities—music lessons, camp, youth orchestras, supportive parents, an instrument to practice on—yet I still didn't make it. Thus the only explanation for not making it was, well, *me*. If I just worked harder (or more deliberately) or had more ambition, first with music and now with writing, I'd be more successful. I just needed to push myself harder, longer, and smarter. I just needed more positive affirmations, more discipline, more optimizing.

Implicit in Adam Grant's yarns about Henry Ford, Stephen King, and the Warby Parker dudes is the idea of grit. Sure, these guys had day jobs for a while, but they grittily persevered and eventually succeeded. It reminds me of that super unsubtle part of the self-help novel *The Alchemist* when the miner is just about to give up and then finds the gem. That could be you, friend, if you *just keep digging.* If you just have enough grit.

My own personal grit and privilege aside, grit as a one-size-fits-all approach to success is pretty problematic. David Denby wrote in *The New Yorker* about how grit may be inaccessible for "some kids all through childhood, and perhaps beyond." Denby quoted Jack Shonkoff, the director of Harvard's Center on the Developing Child:

If you haven't in your early years been growing up in an environment of responsive relationships that has buffered you from excessive stress activation, then if, in tenth-grade math class, you're not showing grit and motivation, it may not be a matter of you just not sucking it up enough. A lot of it has to do with problems of focusing attention, working memory, and cognitive flexibility. And you may not have developed those capacities because of what happened to you early in life.

"Duckworth—indifferent to class, race, history, society, culture—strips success of its human reality," Denby wrote. There are countless examples of how this human reality plays out in the arts. In the UK, artists are mostly from the middle class. A mere 16 percent are from working-class backgrounds. In the United States, Createquity did a recent analysis that found "professionals in 'Arts, design, entertainment, sports, and media occupations' were about 60% more likely than average to have a father who attended at least some college . . . and 70% more likely to have a mother who attended college . . . That is the most extreme skew of any of 23 occupation categories for mother's education; for fathers, it's exceeded only by mathematics and computer science occupations." The average family income of someone who graduates with a BFA is close to $95,000. Low-income students are "less likely to have access to arts education than their higher-income peers." Yet students who do have access to arts education in high school are "three times more likely than students who lacked those experiences to earn a bachelor's degree." The psychologist Mihaly Csikszentmihalyi, who studies creativity, writes that creative contributions require "training, expectations, resources, recognition, hope, opportunity, and reward." And clearly not everyone has equal access to these assets.

We are taught that the heroic thing to do in the face of personal or professional adversity is to persevere. Persist hard enough with the right attitude and the universe will provide, right? Well, maybe, but maybe not. In the meantime, how much psychological and financial uncertainty can you tolerate?

"It's particularly easy for people with economic and social privileges to say, 'Do what you love and the money will follow,'" writes Manjula Martin in the introduction to *Scratch: Writers, Money, and the Art of Making a Living.* "But it's not always so simple for the rest—the people without prestigious degrees or parents standing ready to help with a loan." In addition, we've got significant gender and/or racial diversity problems in music, movies, theater, art museums, publishing houses, and other cultural gatekeepers, which in turn affects how diverse the art is that gets produced, published, and promoted.

The writers who contributed essays to that collection include Alexander Chee, who bluntly states that "there is an illusory 'made it' point, the point at which the writer no longer has to worry about money. It doesn't exist unless you were born someone who didn't ever have to worry about it."

In the same volume, Yiyun Li talks about how cagey Americans are about class: "Americans want to think you can be a self-made man no matter what your background is. But the truth is, actually, whatever class you were born into is more important." You don't have to look any further than the latest college admissions scandal, where wealthy parents bought spots for their kids at elite schools, to implode the myth of the level playing field.

In *Bright-Sided: How the Relentless Promotion of Positive Thinking Has Undermined America* the journalist Barbara Ehrenreich deconstructs the magical-thinking American exceptionalism that inspires us to believe good things happen to good people and failure is the result of a bad attitude. You simply didn't "believe firmly enough in the inevitability of your success." Theorist Jack Halberstam notes in *The Queer Art of Failure* that "believing that success depends on one's attitude is far preferable to Americans than recognizing that their success is the outcome of the tilted scales of race, class, and gender."

Gladwell's, Ericsson's, and Duckworth's works are more nuanced than the sound-bite takeaways that circulate, but if you call a chapter "The 10,000 Hour Rule" without so much as a question mark following it, *of course* that's what people will remember. Simple sells because it's what we so badly want to believe, especially when it comes to our own potential. But potential doesn't exist in a vacuum.

And then there is the most elusive variable of all: luck. Luck is real but difficult to quantify, though some researchers have tried. Take a recent study on the relationship between wealth and luck. Using a computer model, researchers simulated a group of people who all had a certain level of talent (skill, intelligence, etc.). They randomly inserted "lucky events that individuals can exploit to increase their wealth if they are talented enough" as well as "unlucky events that reduce their wealth" over a forty-year period (the average working life). The results mimicked the wealth distribution of what we see in the real world. The researchers found the wealthiest 20 percent of the group were not the most talented. They were the luckiest.

"It is evident that the most successful individuals are also the luckiest ones," one of the paper's coauthors summarized.

If you don't want to take a scientist's word for it, maybe you'll believe a professional gambler. Annie Duke was a championship poker player who now travels around sharing her version of the science of smart decision-making. In an interview with *Nautilus,* she described how the word *resulting* is used in poker:

> It's a really important word. You can think about it as creating too tight a relationship between the quality of the outcome and the quality of the decision . . . In chess, if I lose a game, it's pretty certain that I made a bad decision somewhere and I can go look for it. That's a totally reasonable strategy. But it is a very unreasonable strategy in poker. If I lose a hand, I may have played the hand literally perfectly and still lost

because there's this luck element to it. The problem is that we're all resulters at heart.

I have always treated my life like a chess game—focusing on right or wrong moves and what I believed to be their attendant outcomes—when it turns out a poker game is a much more useful analogy.

"Wrap your arms around the uncertainty," Duke said. "Accept it. Know that the way things turn out has a lot of luck involved so don't be so hard on yourself when things go badly and don't be so proud of yourself when they go well."

ADAM AND his writing partner parted ways about a year before we reconnected. They'd been collaborating since right after college, but after a series of stalled projects like the one they thought was their big break, Adam convinced him to move from New York to L.A.

"We're trying to win a boxing match with one arm," he'd said. "We don't live in the city where it's all happening."

In L.A., things *did* start happening for them. But then Adam's partner decided to try writing a script alone, and that script turned into a star-studded blockbuster. There was even Oscar buzz.

Adam and his partner had equal ambitions, as far as I could tell. They had both worked hard. And yet, despite that, as is often the case, their fortunes had diverged. Based on what, exactly? Talent? Luck? Both?

Tamar must have struggled with this when one of her TV show costars went on to become a household celebrity name. I had been abstractly envious of plenty of other writers, and very concretely jealous of a close friend perpetually one step ahead of me in her career. I could imagine the torrent of dark feelings that might have rushed over me if not only a friend but a former writing partner had experienced the magnitude of success as Adam's had. *I'm the one who brought him out here,* I might have seethed. Maybe even: *It should have been me.*

But apparently Jenna wasn't the only Dalai Lama I was going to encounter on this quest, because Adam and his former partner had remained close friends who continued to support each other's work. And I think it was because Adam understood the complicated nature of these variables and because of his healthy belief that your work doesn't owe you a goddamn thing in return for doing it. Put in your hours, he told himself. The rest is out of your control.

After reckoning with various external influences, we must also do battle with our own psyches. Adam's approach—work hard and leave it to others to decide your artistic fate—was his armor against self-doubt, but that's easier said than done. Everyone I know who makes any kind of art battles an inner critic telling her the work is no good. We struggle with envy. We struggle with fear. We struggle with self-doubt. We struggle with indecisiveness and disappointment and the pressure of what we think our lives and careers *should* look like. We are human beings, not robots, no matter how much internet clickbait tells us we can hack who we are and what we can accomplish. To endure, you must be able to bear hearing these voices or block them out, as well as bear with maybe touching it, then maybe losing it, then maybe touching it again.

The Space Between Wanting and Getting

At Interlochen my friends and I became invested in the arts, and we had sustained that connection into adulthood. But my conversations with Adam made me consider how I would be a little more grounded if I didn't cling quite so tightly to that identity, instead simply putting in the hours. I could benefit from putting some space between ambition and outcome.

A photographer named Tracey Moffatt photographed competitors who came in fourth at the 2000 Olympics. Her goal was to capture the moment they realized they had *just* missed getting a medal. Their expressions are captivating, carefully constructed blank stares where you know something intense is brewing just below the surface. Moffatt summarized it as an "awful, beautiful, knowing mask."

It was difficult to capture these moments, Moffat says, because "the camera always swings past them onto the winner." I wondered if that was the way Tamar thought about her acting career—that she had *almost* medaled. She had been so close. I also wondered if she had any expiration date in mind for putting in more hours and grittily pursuing her passion, or if she was determined to keep going until she touched success again no matter what.

ADAM AND I KEPT in touch. Some months after our first conversation his show was canceled (as are around 65 percent of shows after the first season; approximately 90 percent of them never make it past the pitch stage to air in the first place). Six months after that, another of his TV series was greenlit.

The one constant for Adam was putting in the writing hours no matter what. He always had multiple projects going, never relying on one big break.

"There is no lottery-winning moment," Adam said.

"Are you fulfilled?" I asked him.

"Yes, absolutely. The marker is: Do I like what I'm working on, and do I feel good about what I'm working on? Right now the answer is yes. And that's satisfying. Like anything in life, the good times might be fleeting, but so are the bad times. Right now I really love this job. If you talk to me in six months, it might all have become a mess. But that's the risk you take. You take it every time."

We want our lives to be like the stories and profiles we read: coherent characters, a clear line between cause and effect, linear progress, distinct beginnings and endings, decisive turning points and epiphanies. Of course, we never *really* know where we are in our own story because unlike fiction (and nonfiction, for that matter), our real lives only have one true ending—and unless there is an afterlife, you can't look back from there to make neat sense of all your twists and turns.

There's a quote I like from a commencement speech J. K. Rowling gave at Harvard University. "I am not going to stand here and tell you that failure is fun," the *Harry Potter* writer told the newly minted grads. "That period of my life was a dark one, and I had no idea that there was going to be what the press has since represented as a kind of fairy tale resolution."

It's common internet lore by now that the first Harry Potter book was rejected by twelve publishers before she became an internationally acclaimed author, but what I like is that Rowling takes a moment to recall and acknowledge that part of the pain of that period was in not knowing what would ultimately happen to the work she had poured her energy and love into.

Because the truth is, one's efforts might *never* be rewarded like J. K. Rowling's was, and we deserve only "to work really hard at what we love," as writer/advice columnist Heather Havrilesky put it. That doesn't mean success isn't important, though, especially when it comes to making enough money to continue doing what you love if you're determined to do it for a living. Nobody can decide for us when to stop trying, although others are more than happy to label us successes or failures based on their own definitions of where we are in the plot lines they've projected onto us. Ambition isn't static; like us, it changes over time.

All you can do is pick a path and see where it leads and who you turn into when you walk down it. Sarah, the next person I set out to interview, had been on a path to become a flutist back when we were kids. I wondered if she was still on it.

4

Never Quit! (But Maybe Quit)

Sarah and I were settled on the couch in her cozy Bronx apartment sipping green tea. Jack, her ten-month-old, lounged on the living room rug, methodically licking each of the dozen or so alphabet blocks scattered around. Sarah was telling me about how she had only been playing the flute for six months when she first went to camp. She was nine years old and had gotten very good very fast. Her grandfather, an amateur pianist, had saved up for decades so he could pay for any of his nine grandkids who got into Interlochen, and he paid Sarah's way for six summers.

Before Interlochen, Sarah practiced every day for fifteen minutes. But at camp she started practicing for an hour a day and kept up her new schedule after she got home. If you have ever met a nine-year-old, you will appreciate this Herculean feat of sustained concentration.

At thirty-two, Sarah almost couldn't fathom her disciplined younger self. "Who does that?" she said. "I didn't even know enough songs to play for an entire hour."

Sarah placed third chair in the orchestra during her first week of camp.

"I didn't even know how to play all the notes on my flute. I didn't know the person ahead or below me or even that it was a ranking system. I asked my stand partner in fourth chair how to play a certain passage and she was so mad that I was sitting in front of her and didn't know. And then of course at challenges I fell way behind."

Challenges (aka "Bloody Friday") were weekly competitions between members of the same orchestra section. Here's how it worked. Say there were seven violists. Five turned their backs to preserve anonymity while the other two played the same passage. The five voted on who played better. The victor moved up a chair; the loser moved down. The winner of that round then challenged the player ahead of her. And so on until first chair was decided—at least until the following week. We took challenges *very* seriously, and there was much crying and gloating involved. Even if you were best friends with your stand partner, you woke up Friday morning determined above all else to eviscerate her.

"I realized then that I was pretty competitive because I was like, 'Wait a minute, I started in third chair, and I *need* to get back up there,'" Sarah said. "That's when my drive kicked into overdrive. There was no way I was staying in the back of the section."

Interlochen and ambition were inextricably linked for Sarah. She didn't know if camp had instilled this drive in her or if she had simply tapped into some essential musical ambition that would have eventually emerged one way or another. Unlike Adam, who had described a laid-back, collegial vibe among the Interlochen theater kids, or Jenna, who never seemed fazed by the fierce competition, Sarah remembered camp as cutthroat for musicians.

"There were people monitoring the practice huts to make sure we'd played for long enough," Sarah said. "It was very intense."

Had it not been for the friendships, she thinks the place would have broken a lot of people, including her. Still, like Jenna and me, she credits camp with her desire to pursue a career in the arts.

"I decided at camp I was going to be a musician even if I never made a lot of money," she said. "My dad worked in advertising, and he hated it. I was determined not to end up like him. I was going to do something I loved."

After high school, Sarah majored in performance at Indiana University. Near the end of college, though, her commitment wavered. She rebelled against a strict teacher who wanted her to live in the music majors' dorm instead of with her nonmusician friends. Like Jenna, she craved a social life in college, yet Sarah's omniscient instructor somehow knew every time she went to a party instead of practicing and constantly lectured her about "priorities." Sarah didn't like being told what to do, then or now, and a distaste for authority does not exactly square with being under the tutelage of a music professor.

"After college, I remember saying, 'I'm done. I'm going to take some time and figure out what I want to do, but I'm done.' But my teacher pushed back: 'You're not done. I'm going to put you in touch with some people running a master's program.' I said, 'Fine, but I'm not going anywhere to audition. I'll send a tape.' I was a jerk about it. But then I sent the tape and got an assistantship, so I was going to be paid to do my master's. And I thought, *I've never lived in Louisiana and I'd like to try it out.* And during those two years I started really loving music again. I was in the Baton Rouge Symphony. I was practicing a lot and enjoying it."

As it had at Interlochen, Sarah's drive kicked into overdrive. "It was so easy there," she said. "You can have this position. You can teach this student. Being in the symphony was amazing, and I thought about staying, but I knew that if I stayed, I was going to get stuck."

"What would be so bad about being stuck if you were happy?" I said.

"The Baton Rouge Symphony is a per-service orchestra. You get paid for your time as opposed to being salaried. Some of the smaller orchestras around the country are like that. And even when you put it all together, you need fourteen more jobs. But also, it was just *too* easy. Everything was laid out for me. That's why I moved to New York. I wanted to see what I could *really* accomplish."

In New York, though, Sarah ended up a freelance musician in per-service music ensembles with even less stability than she'd had in the Baton Rouge Symphony Orchestra. And this time she was in a city no one has ever described as "too easy."

The Gig Economy Musician

Cobbling together a living from multiple sources is nothing new for musicians. Even salaried orchestra musicians often teach private lessons to supplement their income. The *gig* in the phrase *gig economy* is pulled straight from the musician's world. Jazz players popularized the term to refer to club dates or jobs, especially a one-night engagement. One of the meanings of *gig* as a verb is "to work as a musician."

Now we use *gig* for contract and freelance jobs of all sorts. We're supposed to be scrappy and build our personal brands as we hawk guitar lessons on Fiverr and necklaces on Etsy, drive for Uber and cook for Feastly, adjunct teach and play in per-service orchestras. We're supposed to work harder, longer, and cheaper than our parents. We're supposed to be nicer, too, because god forbid we lose a starred rating for any of the services we're providing or utilizing. We're supposed to disrupt and innovate and influence and make art—oh, and we also need to be popular enough on Twitter and Instagram to sell it.

In the years since Sarah and I graduated, it's become more and more difficult for musicians. In 2011, my hometown orchestra filed for bankruptcy, along with major orchestras in Philadelphia and Honolulu. There have been strikes and labor battles and pay freezes, and orchestra attendance continues to drop. Orchestras operating with a deficit are nothing new, but in 2016 *The New York Times* proclaimed: "It's Official: Many Orchestras Are Now Charities":

While orchestras have always required subsidies—whether from monarchs, the church, governments or patrons—the balance has shifted to the point where they generally get more revenue from donations than from selling tickets, according to a report . . . by the League of American Orchestras . . . The report also found that orchestras had reached a tipping point in how they sell tickets: In 2013, for the first time, ensembles no longer earned a majority of their ticket revenue from the subscription packages they have depended on for decades.

The flutist Alice Jones wrote on her website about what this reality means for individual musicians:

There are 117 symphony orchestras in the US. That means there are approximately 11,700 orchestral job positions in the US, assuming each orchestra has 100 players, which is an over-estimate. But that's not the same as saying there are 11,700 job openings there are every year, because once someone wins a good orchestral job, they hold on to it for 30–40 years. For flute players, for example, there were only 4 job openings in the US in all of 2015–16.

Four job openings in one year for flutists like Sarah. Four! Those are some incredibly tough odds.

Sarah wasn't the only one understandably stressed out

by making it as a musician. In a study of over two thousand professional musicians, for example, 69 percent reported symptoms of depression at some time in their career. Some 71 percent believed that they had experienced panic attacks or high levels of anxiety. Two of the report's most harrowing takeaways: "whereas artists find solace in the production of music, the working conditions of forging a musical career are traumatic," and "music making is therapeutic, but making a career out of music is destructive."

When I think of the gig economy we're all part of now, artists and nonartists alike, I think of the essay "Slouching Towards Bethlehem," in which Joan Didion profiles the runaways, activists, and philosophers who populated the Haight-Ashbury district in the late 1960s. Whereas the press depicted a colorful counterculture, Didion saw something different: a community of "pathetically unequipped children." They were unequipped to deal with the world, Didion argues, because "[a]t some point between 1945 and 1967 we had somehow neglected to tell these children the rules of the game we happened to be playing. Maybe we had stopped believing in the rules ourselves, maybe we were having a failure of nerve about the game."

In the last few decades, the rules have changed yet again. "For Americans under the age of 40, the 21st century has resembled one long recession," writes the journalist David Leonhardt. We have more debt than our parents. We own fewer homes. We will retire later and probably with less savings. Ninety-two percent of thirty-year-olds born in 1940 had higher earnings (adjusted for inflation) than their parents. Ninety-two percent! Baby boomers had all the economic reasons in the world to be optimistic when they entered the workforce, but in the late 1980s economic inequality began to rise, thanks to globalization, new technologies, government policies favoring those with more money, and a slowdown in educational attainment. These shifts negatively affected the middle class and poor. The tech boom of the nineties temporarily hit the pause button on economic decline, but we all know how that story ends. For those born in 1980, "only half of them make as much money as their parents did."

The journalist Scott Timberg has written how this has affected America's creative class, a term coined by the urban studies theorist Richard Florida. Timberg has described how hard hit the creative industries were during the Bush years and the Great Recession—the years my friends and I came of age—but he argues that less attention has been paid to the loss of creative jobs than to job attrition in other fields because we don't realize that most artists are working-class people. Forget the fabulously successful musicians and actors who get the most press; the majority of artists are freelancers cobbling together multiple gigs. Despite often having college degrees, they typically make less than the average professional.

I emailed Timberg and asked if we should even be encouraging young people to try to make a career in the arts given how difficult it is, especially considering the free-content digital culture we live in now, which many believe is crushing "creator wages."

"Much of the economic infrastructure that supported the arts has collapsed, and the internet has only restored that scaffolding in isolated patches," he wrote back. "I'd hate to discourage anyone from pursuing the arts or writing or whatever, but those who do need to go in with their eyes open to the risk and the ways these fields have changed."

Add to these concrete economic realities the subjective nature of art.

"You know how it is," Sarah said. "It's somebody's opinion about your playing once you get past playing wrong notes. Right before I quit, the conductor of one of the chamber groups I was in just didn't like the way I played. She pretty much had me removed from the orchestra. We were going on tour and she had one of my friends replace me. I thought, *Why am I struggling so much financially to be at the whim of somebody's opinion?*"

"What about not caring about money because you were doing what you love?" I said.

"But I didn't love it anymore," she said. "I hated it, just like my dad had hated his advertising job."

I thought back to how kid me had imagined her adult life as a musician, carrying my viola on the subway to rehearsals, strangers knowing when they saw me with my instrument: there goes an artist pursuing her passion. Nowhere in that fuzzy childhood fantasy was potential money stress or the exhaustion of crisscrossing the city multiple times a day for rehearsals and performances, or conductors deciding they didn't like me or my playing.

I had spent such a crazy amount of time trying to figure out how I could possibly have failed at the thing I loved that I hadn't even bothered questioning this fantasy. Given my obsession as a kid with moving to New York City, I probably would have ended up in a similar version of Sarah's life as a musician. (And that's based on the bold assumption I made it that far.) I can't imagine I would have thrived in a freelance musician's world. After all, I had recently taken a part-time day job because I realized I needed more financial stability than I was able to get as a freelance writer.

"We have to be attentive . . . to what we use fantasy to do; whether it becomes, as we say, an end in itself," writes psychotherapist Adam Phillips. My musician's life fantasy *had* become an end in itself. I could see that now. It was a way for me to escape into the past during moments I had doubts or insecurities about my present.

Sarah had put in her ten thousand hours. She had grit. And she was miserable. I'd told myself that my misery studying music in college was par for the course for an artist. But we are not required to suffer, not even artists. Sarah was wise enough to know that.

SARAH QUIT THE FLUTE when she was twenty-nine. She had finished a doctorate in music by then but decided not to teach.

"I thought about myself in college, how my teacher had

to struggle so much to get me to keep going. I ended up really dedicated to the flute again after college, but I realized that teaching kids who weren't into music would have been too painful after it had meant so much to me."

With no teacher urging her to keep going, this time she was really done.

"So you don't play at all now?" I asked.

"No, never," she said. "Never." She glanced in the direction of a hall closet. "But it's funny, I guess I didn't want to be *done* done because I haven't sold my flute or my piccolo."

I thought of my viola taking up valuable closet space in my 250-square-foot bedroom. I assumed that hanging on to her flute meant Sarah was conflicted, like me, but when I asked if she was happy with her decision, she didn't hesitate.

"Absolutely," she said. "There's a piece of me still connected to the flute, but I'm very clear that it's not at all what I want to do."

After the flute, Sarah went back to school for a degree in early education and started teaching at a progressive elementary school in the Bronx.

"It's super hands-on learning. There are no books, but you learn by going out and doing. Now my teaching philosophy is the opposite of Interlochen. *What do you think?* instead of *This is the way it is.* It's such an awesome environment. After I got my master's, I started implementing different sound curriculum. What you hear tells you a lot about where you are. I have them sit outside and close their eyes and tell me what they hear: birds chirping, people chatting, dogs barking. It took me a minute to spin it and realize I can still incorporate music or the arts in some way."

She did wonder what might have happened had she chosen a different school for her doctorate. If she had gone to Texas, maybe it would have been like Louisiana—she would have gotten more positive feedback and continued to put her all into it.

"But this is my destiny for sure," she said. "This is where I needed to be to figure it all out."

"We tell ourselves stories in order to live," as Joan Didion put it, and writers of all people understand the concept of spin. Jenna's spin was about balance. Adam's was to focus on process over outcome. Sarah's spin was destiny. And then there was *my* depressing spin. I had absorbed the idea that even if I was miserable, I should persevere no matter what, because "you never fail until you stop trying." Quitting music meant I lacked grit. When the going got tough, I couldn't hack it. My spin was *failure*.

On Failure

When I say failure, I'm not talking about the everyday rejections that come with trying to make a living in the arts (and in many fields). I had bounced back from many a mediocre audition when I was younger, and music had thickened my skin enough that when as a freelance writer I started pitching my ideas to editors, I (mostly) didn't take it personally when they were rejected. I just moved on to the next publication and tried again. And of course making art is in itself a daily lesson in failure because that Ira Glass gap never fully closes.

But the moments I had experienced major disappointment in my adult life—quitting the viola, getting divorced, having my second book rejected—the moments where I was forced to modify the Grand Vision for my life, well, that was another story. "Follow your dreams," we're told, with not a whole lot of substantive advice about how to handle things not working out as planned.

College administrators have lately noticed they're inheriting cohorts of stressed-out perfectionistic failure failures who need help coping with life's setbacks. It's why Smith College now has a series of workshops on "Failing Well." Harvard has its Success-Failure Project showcasing stories of rejection, while University of Texas students can log in to an app called Thrive aimed at easing the stressful "ups and downs of campus life." In an article in *The New York Times,* Jessica Bennett wrote about these and other projects, with revealing quotes from high-achieving students:

> "We all came from high schools where we were all the exception to the rule—we were kind of special in some way, or people told us that," said Cai Sherley, 20, seated in the campus café . . . "So you get here and of course you want to recreate that," Ms. Sherley said. "But here, everybody's special. So nobody is special."

Everybody's special, so nobody's special. That's quite the mindfuck after eighteen years of high achievement, outsize expectations, self-esteem boosting, and the pressure of potential. It no doubt partly explains why experts are sounding the alarm about a growing mental health crisis among college students. In a survey of 275 counseling centers, 94 percent of directors report that recent trends toward a greater number of students with severe psychological problems continue to be true on their campuses. The vast majority of them noted increases in anxiety disorders over the past five years. And anxiety is the most common concern among students (48.2 percent). Heather Havrilesky writes in her latest book about fielding questions from millennials that reveal these kinds of anxieties: "dispatches from young people who feel guilty and inadequate at every turn and who compare themselves relentlessly to others."

No matter our stereotypes of suffering artists, I'd venture to argue that feeling constantly guilty and inadequate and anxious isn't great for making art, or for anything that requires experimentation, vulnerability, confidence, or sustained focus. It seems to be getting harder and harder for everyone (but maybe for those under thirty, those who grew up online, most of all) to cope with failure thanks to the potent mix of "you can do anything!" messaging combined with gig economy realities and social media constantly clamoring for us to perform and compare our achievements. And then when we do have setbacks, we're not encouraged to reflect on them and consider that maybe something really has been lost (a goal, an idea about who we are) and that this is a natural part of life. Instead, we're supposed to immediately rebrand every failure as a learning opportunity spurring us on to our next great challenge.

THE AMERICAN concept of failure has an interesting history. Before the Civil War, *failure* was a term reserved for failed businesses. It meant "breaking in business" (i.e., going broke). In the nineteenth century, *failure* and other terms from finance slowly shifted from being ways people talked about their businesses to being ways they talked about themselves. Failure has become more than something that a person experiences; it has become an identity. The historian Scott Sandage argues that by the twentieth century there had been a definitive transformation: now the concept of failure conjures up not merely lost business but also lost souls (because today, what we do for a living is who we are).

Sandage writes:

> We reckon our incomes once a year but audit ourselves daily, by standards of long-forgotten origin. Who thinks of the old counting house when we "take stock" of how we "spend" our lives, take "credit" for our gains, or try not to end up "third rate" or "good for nothing"? Someday, we hope, "the bottom line" will show that we "amount to something." By this kind of talk we "balance" our whole lives, not just our accounts.

Feeling disappointed about something not working out is not the same as feeling disappointed in yourself. Experiencing failure is not the same as feeling like a failure. That, I realized, was the psychic line I had walked across somewhere along the way, and I needed to cross back over to the other side.

I was taught that the biggest bludgeon I had to beat back failure was perseverance. Like Tennyson's adventure-addicted Ulysses, I should strive, seek, find, and never yield. Quoth the Pinterest Churchillians: "Never give in. Never give in. Never, Never, Never, Never—in nothing, great or small, large or petty . . ." Of course, often left out of Churchill's speech to his alma mater are the lines that follow: ". . . never give in, except to convictions of honour and good sense." Those are some pretty sizable exceptions.

We're taught as kids to keep our commitments. Play the whole season. Practice fifteen minutes a day. Show up for your weekly study group. Commitment is a good skill to cultivate, but maybe we should also have a mandatory class for all high school seniors or college freshmen about how to gracefully quit something you've given a good go and no longer want to invest in. It would offer up strategies for how to disentangle yourself from your kid ambitions, how to stop comparing yourself to other people, and how to accept failure and loss as part of growing up. It would emphasize it's okay to take time to self-reflect instead of thinking your understandable disappointment requires immediate self-help intervention.

Quitting in the arts is especially fraught, because there is this idea that if you quit, you were never a Real Artist in the first place. Quitting is supposed to be for soul-sucking day jobs, not for those who are following their dreams. Professional artists are the lucky ones who get to make a living doing what they love, whereas everyone else had to grow up and get a "real" job.

A Real Artist keeps doing what she loves "whether it causes a stir or not." Maybe you're thinking that's what happened with Sarah. She kept going with music for a while because she was talented and received positive feedback and because it was relatively easy. But praise and progress *matter* to our psyches. They obviously shouldn't be one's sole motivation—and they weren't Sarah's—but without them, it eventually and understandably gets tough for many of us to keep going.

Also, pursuing something that comes at least somewhat naturally makes sense despite how much we love to focus on how a difficult task is the only worthwhile one and how the only true failure is giving up. Giving up is seen as a character flaw these days, no matter the endeavor. The mentality that we can achieve anything with enough hard work and that we have a moral obligation to try, try, and try again is part and parcel of the American dream. But such perseverance is pathological.

Sarah quit because she felt more frustrated than fulfilled. She quit because she no longer felt joyful making music. Professionalizing her passion had changed that. Of *course* that can happen. And when it did, she knew, as Nina Simone counseled, that "you have to learn to get up from the table when love is no longer being served."

I tend to downplay in my mind the fact that before I quit viola, it wasn't going well at *all*. I was sick to my stomach with anxiety before lessons; I was so obsessively focused on getting better that I was getting worse. Also, the truth is, like Jenna and Sarah, I wanted to do more than just eat, sleep, and practice. I had other burgeoning interests, including writing. Yet I still couldn't fully let go of the feeling of failure for falling short of my own expectations and out of love with what was supposed to be the driving passion for my life.

OVER THE YEARS I've tried reframing my relationship to feelings of disappointment and failure by reading spiritual authors like Eckhart Tolle and Louise Hay. I'm as tempted as the next neurotic New Yorker by anyone who comes along promising serenity through nonattachment, affirmations, and positively manifesting my destiny.

But . . . I don't know. Somewhere along the way I always get frustrated by the premise that we have a mind-over-matter relationship with everything from our illnesses to our love lives to our finances. I don't want to be a victim of my circumstances, but surely I don't have control over *everything*.

And as much as I'm drawn in theory to the idea of nonattachment, it doesn't feel like a realistic or necessarily even desirable goal. I'd rather cultivate what philosopher Todd May calls a "slightly less lacerating vulnerability."

Obviously, I care about the projects and people I put my love and energy into, and that means caring about the outcome of that effort. Oprah once asked Eckhart Tolle if he was serene 24/7 or if he ever felt intense emotions. (I'm summarizing.) He told her that while he enjoyed his life, he no longer ever got "excited." Um, thanks but no thanks. I'm quite attached to being able to feel excitement.

Americans are encouraged to practice what journalist Barbara Ehrenreich calls "relentless optimism." Ruth Whippman echoes this sentiment: "The real problems in our lives are never discrimination or poverty, bad relationships or unfair bosses . . . but our own failure to . . . think positive or practice mindfulness, to 'take personal responsibility' or 'count our blessings.'" If you're disappointed in any part of your adult life in this "positive thinking, power of attraction, simple formula for success" cultural moment we find ourselves in, well, that's on you, friend . . .

That relentless optimism has also found a home in Silicon Valley. In start-up culture, you don't fail. You take necessary risks and gambles on your way to greatness. Shoot for the stars, and if you miss (and 90 percent of start-ups miss), well, it's just one more learning opportunity. That's why we've got books like *The Up Side of Down: Why Failing Well Is the Key to Success*; *Adapt: Why Success Always Starts with Failure*; *Failing Forward: Turning Mistakes into Stepping Stones for Success*. Fail up. Fail smart. Fail forward. Poor Samuel Beckett's out-of-context "Fail again. Fail better" quote is bandied about so aggressively on Twitter by Burning Man–going, Bulletproof coffee–drinking, productivity-hacking tech bros that you might mistakenly think Beckett was a motivational speaker and not a depressed Irish nihilist.

WE DON'T LIKE to talk about the experience of disappointment. We see it as negativity, as not spinning your failure as opportunity, as breaking the Faustian pact of Instagram-filtered perfection, or as questioning the fundamental American belief in the cause-and-effect relationship between hard work and reward. Get your vision board. Get your gratitude journal. Get your can-do attitude and mantras and wash your face, girl.

The American Tibetan Buddhist Pema Chödrön has a variation of Beckett's "fail better" I like much more than Silicon Valley's: "'Fail better' means you begin to have the ability to hold . . . 'the rawness of vulnerability' in your heart, and see it as your connection with other human beings and as a part of your humanness." Most of us don't like feeling vulnerable; our impulse is to run away from that feeling. "Can you allow yourself to feel what you feel when things don't go the way you want them to?" Chödrön asks. These are moments when we feel disappointment or insecurity or heartbreak or failed expectations. Failing well means accepting those feelings instead of lashing out by blaming ourselves or others. It means cultivating some curiosity about what you are feeling and why you're feeling that way.

Quitting viola *was* a kind of failure, in that I failed to

achieve a thing I had set out to. But quitting was also an understandable choice I made within the context of being miserable. I wanted to be able to make space for the disappointment I'd felt about not becoming a musician without being so hard on myself. I'd never really done this. It felt silly to give the disappointment room, like I was indulging in mourning the loss of a childish fantasy. It also felt silly to grieve the loss of my musician self when I had ended up with a writing self. But that's kind of like saying someone who is happily remarried shouldn't ever feel loss or regret or wonder what had gone wrong when she thinks about her first marriage.

Disappointment lives in the space between wanting and getting, and we're taught that where there's a will, there's a way, so the only person to blame if you're in that liminal space is yourself. And yet it's such a common human experience not to get what you want—maybe the most universal of all experiences.

How about some books where we focus on gracefully giving up on something? Or books that celebrate the freedom of letting go of our dreams and moving on to something else where we won't have to beat our heads against the wall? Or books that say it's natural sometimes to hit the limits of our ambition, talent, or desire? How about we stop telling people that they failed because they weren't determined enough or didn't believe in themselves enough? Sure, sometimes that's true. But not all the time. Maybe not even most of the time. There must be some middle ground between cynicism and optimism when it comes to failure, a space where we can have compassion for our own failures without becoming victim to them but also without needing to mythologize them as a mere stop on the way to success. There must be some warmhearted realistic view we could take of our own setbacks and frustrations without anchoring our identities to them.

A self-help book would probably encourage me to reframe failure as a conscious choice, part of my transformation into a writer. And this is partially true. But I sensed it was less useful for me to deny the idea of failure than to learn how to distance my ego from it. I wanted to feel okay that I had failed to become what I'd envisioned. I wanted to give space to my capital F failures, and then I wanted to let them go.

IN 2004, *The New York Times* published a piece that checked in with thirty-six former Juilliard graduates ten years later:

At least 12 are out of professional music performance. Eleven have full-time orchestra jobs. Another, a cellist, recently quit the Hong Kong Philharmonic to move back in with his parents in Dayton, Ohio, and audition for American orchestra jobs. Four are freelancers who survive by teaching; five more consider themselves full-time freelancers or chamber musicians; three consider themselves mainly soloists.

I think about this article from time to time. It came out six months after I graduated from college. My dad mailed it to me in Sydney, Australia, where I was waitressing and backpacking and loving being 15,000 miles away from having to decide what to do with my adult life. He sent me the article to make me feel better about quitting viola. He wanted to show me how hard it was to make it in the arts, even for those who attended the best music school in the country.

There were three violists in my freshman class at college. I was the first to quit, but the other two both changed their majors from music by junior year. Amy now works in marketing, and Lena is a high school biology teacher. But none of that reality-check information had made a dent in my feelings of failure, so strongly ingrained was the belief that I should have persevered no matter what.

It was a revelation to me that Sarah could quit music and not feel like a failure. I was tempted to chalk this up to the fact that she made it further than I did. She had been a "real" working musician, whereas I had quit in college. She had gone the distance with her career and decided it wasn't what she wanted, while I had always thought of myself as quitting before I had really tested myself.

But let me try out Sarah's destiny spin for a second. New York was Sarah's testing ground, but college was mine. Maybe that's as far as I was meant to go. The next step was to forgive myself for the path being shorter than I had imagined. For it being harder to walk down than I had anticipated. I didn't have a teacher urging me on like Sarah and

Jenna did. In fact, I had a teacher who had been much less enthusiastic about my progress. He didn't tell me to quit, but he didn't try to dissuade me when I finally did, either.

"Do you think of nothing else except music?" he had once asked me.

"Yes," I lied, and I knew he'd noticed me hesitate.

Another time he randomly brought up a student of his who had gone on to have a very successful career as a lawyer. I'd thought he was preparing me for the challenging life I'd chosen, but in retrospect I think he saw me cracking under the pressure and was trying to get me to realize there were other options. I didn't have to keep miserably slogging along.

I have given my music school days the romantic gloss of the suffering artist, but the reality is that I was literally sick to my stomach most of the time. My shoulders and back ached constantly. My entire body was screaming at me to quit. There has got to be some distinction between the kind of resistance you can persevere through as part of your tale of triumph and the kind that indicates you've had enough and it's time to head in another direction (ideally one where you don't puke up your breakfast once a week).

Persevering to close the Ira Glass gap is great counsel for beginners, as is Elizabeth Gilbert's *Big Magic* advice not to let fear get in the way of creating art, and Ericsson's to put in your ten thousand hours of deliberate practice. But a million tiny cracks can chip away at your resolve long past the beginner stage. The overbearing Leopold Mozart, father to Wolfgang Amadeus, supposedly exhorted his son to "Be Caesar or be nothing." But we're not all Mozart (or J. K.

Rowling or the Beatles or Philip Glass or Elizabeth Gilbert). When you're in the middle of the pack in your chosen career, when you've gotten some of what you wanted but not enough to make a living doing what you love, quitting as opposed to persevering is murkier territory.

Sarah trusted her own judgment. And quitting made space for something more fulfilling to her than being a musician. There was something revolutionary to me about Sarah saying, "No, enough, this creative career I once wanted because I thought it would be fulfilling turned out not to be, and I'm not going to beat my head against a wall persevering."

This is the flip side of the soul-sucking cubicle-dweller jobs we assume are where dreams go to die. All those books aimed at convincing you to go follow your passion are based on the assumption that if you do so, your life will automatically be more fulfilling. But then let's say you become an entrepreneur or hit the road with your band or land a gig writing guidebooks that takes you all over the world. You can still discover that—gasp!—it's not all it's cracked up to be. Being fulfilled is all about the day-to-day details, and if that involves schlepping your instrument from one gig to another in order to cobble together a living, it may be that there is no piece of chamber music beautiful enough to save you from your misery. And then you have to be smart enough to change course instead of clinging to some idea of yourself or the thing you wanted.

It takes grit to persevere, but sometimes it also takes grit to quit, especially when you've wandered pretty far down a path—when you've tied your identity to walking that path in a world where our primary yardstick for measuring success is longevity. The marriage of twenty years that ends in divorce is a failure. The child star who grew up to become a social worker is featured on some "where are they now?" segment, as if she had disappeared off the face of the earth. It takes courage to quit something you've built your identity around.

The psychology professor Carsten Wrosch has found in his research that people like Sarah who are "better able to let go when they experience unattainable goals" have "less depressive symptoms, less negative affect over time. They also have lower cortisol levels, and they have lower levels of systemic inflammation, which is a marker of immune function. And they develop fewer physical health problems over time." But it's not always obvious when exactly a goal becomes unattainable, to know when to keep striving and when to quit. Wrosch says people make two different kinds of mistakes: "They can quit too early when they should have persisted or they can quit too late."

This was something I had struggled with a lot in thinking about music school. On the one hand, the economist Steven Levitt would say it was a good thing that I had failed fast at viola and could move on to other goals. On the other hand, I fretted over whether quitting made me a quitter. I was also prone to wishful thinking: if only I had started lessons younger, or had practiced more, or had more musical parents, or had gone to a different music school. If, if, if.

In the end, we're the only ones who really know when we've tried hard enough for long enough, if quitting is a strategic choice or a pattern we need to break, despite whatever spin someone else might put on our stories.

Remember those photographs of Olympians who came in fourth place? The photographer said she was trying to show that it was "beautiful to try." It *is* beautiful to try, but there is beauty in quitting, too, because it takes guts to let go of who you thought you were or what you thought you would achieve. Quitting is giving up the known for the unknown. What's braver than that?

I ASKED SARAH if she would encourage her son, Jack, to play an instrument.

"No, I wouldn't," she said. "My husband, who isn't a musician, wants him to, and I wouldn't hold him back, but deep down I think I would be bummed if he chose music because I just know that it's a tough life."

"Financially?" I said.

"Financially, yes. But a bigger part of it is that I want him to love it and not have that feeling like . . . I don't know . . . I don't love music the way I did before. Maybe I got a little jaded. I got to a point where it frustrated me more than anything else. I don't want him to feel that way. I want him to love it and be excited about it. But that's for him to decide."

"What if he wanted to go to Interlochen?" I said.

"I'd totally support him in that. I would love to go back."

I didn't ask Sarah to explain this seeming contradiction. It was the same kind of inner conflict I'd felt watching Jenna's students, hoping the talented ones were going to pursue a career in music while also worrying about what would happen to them if they did. We of course want others to love the thing we loved—we know what joy it can bring—while simultaneously hoping to spare them the pain of potential frustration and disappointment that might accompany it. And, as a parent, Sarah must know that there is some amount of encouraging and pushing to be done, yet also must wonder how to instill the ideal balance of grit and flexibility. Whatever Yo-Yo Ma's musical parents did played a part in him loving the cello, while Andre Agassi's overbearing father pushed him to excel at a sport he's said he hates.

Sarah's parents told her to go for it. Mine did, too. Sure, they voiced concerns that it might be difficult to make a living at music, but they wanted us to do what we loved, and we were determined. So what was Sarah's job with Jack? To tell him to dream big? To sober him up? To say: Work hard for as long as it takes to see a project through in a way that feels satisfying, keep going after that if you still feel driven and fulfilled, and quit if you don't? Above all, make room for "honour and good sense"?

I sat down on the floor next to Jack.

"Will you have the rage to master, little dude?" I asked Jack with my eyes.

"Stop projecting, lady," he told me with his. He stuck his thumb in his mouth and rolled onto his back.

"Time for a nap," Sarah said. She put down her tea and picked him up. "To be continued."

5

Freedom's Just Another Word

Now that she'd reached the end of her journey as a professional musician, Sarah was thinking of quitting New York, too. The city was where she had wanted to test herself, and she had. But she could teach anywhere, and now that she had Jack, she wanted to move closer to her siblings in Memphis.

A handful of my close friends had recently left the city, a few back to their home states and one to her Canadian motherland. They had moved ostensibly to be closer to grandparents who could pitch in with the babies they planned to have. But growing tired of New York—the cost, the noise, the jostling, the lines, the roommates, the walk-ups, the endless striving—was part of it, too. My friends and I all moved here in our twenties, drawn to New York like scores of ambitious, adventurous, scrappy kids before us. But having a fling with New York is totally different than building a life in the city, and we were all considering our future relationship status.

As a child, I spent a lot of time fantasizing about moving to Manhattan, where I would finally start my grown-up artist's life. I'd live in a crumbling loft on the Lower East Side with my roommate, an aspiring actress. Every day she'd head off to auditions and I'd write in the sunlit kitchen or at a local café; at night we'd sit out on the fire escape, drink wine, and talk about books and movies and bad dates.

New York City was where middle-class suburban Jewish girls with artists' souls went to finally be liberated from having to please parents and teachers. It was where the musicians and writers I loved—Bob Dylan, Patti Smith, Dylan Thomas, James Baldwin, John Lennon, Willa Cather—had played and written and gotten drunk. The city was synonymous with self-expression and independence. I had always felt like a misfit growing up, and New York loomed in my imagination as a place where I could finally be myself, whoever that turned out to be—the same way I'd felt free at Interlochen to be creative, quirky, and experimental.

LIKE ME, Eli moved to New York from somewhere else. He's originally from Philadelphia, the son of a practical-minded software engineer mom and a passion-driven musician turned music professor dad. It was Jenna who first connected us via Facebook.

"He was so cute," she said the day we were flipping through photo albums in Chicago. "He was always on his skateboard, he was kind of punk but also really nice, and he drew these awesome comics. I'm going to try and find him." Within minutes she had his profile up: "I sent him a friend request!"

The internet told us that Eli worked at the music website Pitchfork. Or at least he had. It seemed as though he might have left recently. There was a reel on Vimeo of film and TV clips he had edited: footage of concerts and clips of documentaries with oddball subjects like a passionate cat photographer. Jenna's phone chimed while we were watching.

"Friend request accepted!" she said.

ELI AND I MET up for dinner at Pete's Tavern in Gramercy. He still had shaggy blond hair and now a beard to match. We hadn't been close at camp, and at first Eli's reserved demeanor had the whiff of someone who isn't quite sure how weird it is that a girl he barely knew had looked him up after twenty years. Which, honestly, fair enough.

But the more we talked, the more he seemed to settle into being the subject of journalistic inquiry. Eli was a visual artist at camp; as a kid, he loved drawing comic books. I asked him to describe to me his earliest artistic memories, and he told me that when he was around seven years old, he started drawing all his favorite comic book characters: the Hulk, Spider-Man, all of the Marvel Universe. His friends loved to draw, too. They'd get into "draw battles," something I'd never heard of.

"Like, one boy would draw a tank with six guys and rockets and another guy would battle him by creating an even more elaborate tank with more guys and more rockets," he said.

In third grade, Eli discovered Fat Jack's Comicrypt,

Philly's oldest comic book store, two blocks from his elementary school.

"I was like, 'What *is* this? This is *amazing*.' Comics were pretty cheap back then. I used to get fifty cents a day to buy lunch. I would buy comics instead. I was really into collecting shit as a kid. I still have all my comics in three big boxes. I used to have them all super organized. They're still all in their plastic wrappers."

"Did you parents encourage your drawing?" I asked.

"Yes, absolutely," he said. "I did some classes at Moore College's school of art when I was really young. My aunt taught printmaking at Interlochen, so that's how we knew about it. I loved camp. It was mostly musicians and actors and then just a few of us in visual arts. We did lots of figure drawing and landscapes, and of course printmaking with my aunt. And then I'd go back home and focus on comics again."

"Did you want to draw comics professionally?"

"I did, yeah. I wanted to be a penciler. Someone who does the actual drawing. There is the letterer, the penciler, and the inker. I was like, 'Who would want to be a fucking inker? You draw in pencil and someone comes in and inks over the pencil drawings. It's just tracing everything.' The older I got, the more I realized what an art that is. As a kid, though, I was like, 'That's bullshit.' I thought if you can't really draw, you become an inker."

It was a throwaway comment, but it made me think again about how as kids we get such firm ideas in our heads of what we want to do as adults, based on so little information.

Eli gave up drawing in college, though. He had a "big pond, small fish" moment, like me. But what struck him more than that was the realization he wasn't working very hard.

"Were you disappointed to give it up?" I asked.

"No," he said. "I was more frustrated with myself. Why am I such a half-asser?"

There's that idea of grit again, of persevering as a principle, of disappointment in ourselves for not living up to our own expectations. Since I was an outsider looking in on Eli's choices and trajectory, I could see it so much more compassionately than I could my choices with music. Maybe Eli *was* half-assing it, but maybe the half-assing was a sign that he didn't want to draw for a living. He wanted to do something else. He just didn't know what that was yet. This is a confusing moment for those of us who have an early and intense interest. It can be disorienting when you thought you'd nailed so early on that graduation commencement advice to pursue your passion only to realize you've got more exploring and experimenting to do, after all.

"What did you end up majoring in?"

"I went to Gallatin, where you can design your own liberal arts major. I did some visual arts, some Spanish. I took poli sci classes. I had really very little sense of how anything I was learning was going to help me at all."

After college, Eli moved to California and worked in cafés and bars. He did paralegal work once he got tired of the long hours and low wages of the service industry, but he got sick of that, too.

"I came back east when I was twenty-four and stayed at my grandfather's place for a while, which was a real nadir. He lives in a Philly suburb and I lived above his garage. I was there for eight or nine months and working in another restaurant and every day wondering, *What am I going to do with my life?*"

Eli applied to law school just to do *something*. He got in and geared himself up to go. His mom thought it was a good, practical idea; his dad thought he shouldn't do something he didn't love. A few weeks before the semester started, he abruptly decided not to go and instead took a job in his aunt's art gallery in Manhattan.

"They sold Niedermaier furniture, art deco furniture, and antique Chinese art," he said. "It was not at all cool art. They would sell couches for $45,000. They had desks for $200,000. I did a lot of moving, hauling really heavy armoires up and down the Upper East Side. You're dealing with really rich people and their decorators all the time."

Eli worked at the gallery for a year and a half. While he was there, he started going out at night to shoot video of local Brooklyn bands. He recorded Suckers, Chairlift, Mixel Pixel, It Lives, Beluga, the Acrylics, No Age, and also a bunch of up-and-coming bands that have disappeared with barely an internet trace.

Eli bought himself a little handheld camera, and his parents gave him some money to buy a second camera. This was before everyone had smartphones. He'd set up multi-camera shoots at the show. He didn't know what he was doing, but he learned something new every time he went to a show or shot a band at their practice space. And he was having a great time.

"I was like, 'I'll make a website and put up all these great recordings of shows,'" he said. So he quit the gallery to focus full time on creating the site, one that would document the music scene, at least until his small savings ran out.

"Of course I didn't know what I was doing so they're pretty shitty."

"What happened with it?" I asked.

"I'd hired my cousin's boyfriend, who ended up building a site that looked really bad," he said. "It was not what I'd asked for. It wasn't working.

"We'd set a date for the website launch: April 7. But I didn't think we were going to make it. And then with a week to go, Pitchfork announced it was going to launch on April 7. I was like, 'I cannot compete with that.' I said to my girlfriend. 'I think I'm fucked, but maybe I can get a job there.'"

And that's exactly what happened.

The Restless Director/Editor

"I was at Pitchfork for five years," he said. "But I went freelance in 2013. I got sick of only doing music-related stuff."

"What do you work on now?" I said.

"Lots of different stuff. I'm editing a cooking show web series for the *Times* and about to start work on a travel documentary for Vice. And there are other cool random projects of my own, like I'm working on a documentary about this huge Eminem fan. He's this very intense and fascinating French dude who calls himself Silk Shady. He dresses like Em. He makes all these weird videos online. He'll do entire videos where he is showing off all his Em clothes and posters."

"Do you have plenty of work?"

"So far. My benchmark was always: if I make any more than I did at Pitchfork, then I'm good. And I have the past two years. It's much easier to make rent now and I can work from home, work whenever I want."

"Do you find it difficult to balance your own projects with the freelance work?" I asked Eli.

"Yeah, sometimes. My own work always takes a back seat to whatever is paying. I got some advice early on that you should never say no to stuff the first few years unless you have to, and that has served me well. I want to focus on the better projects, but I'm not quite at a place where that's an option. But I'm getting closer to a place where I can say no."

The "whenever, wherever" part of freelance writing is what had appealed to me, too. It was part of that bohemian New Yorker writer's life I had envisioned. Not that free-lancing had been as free as I had pictured it in my head. I spent an inordinate amount of time each month chasing down payments from publications. I worked long hours while constantly worrying I'd run out of work. In reality, I was far from psychically, financially, or artistically free. *Freedom* is one of those words we throw around a lot as an abstract aspiration, but it becomes really complicated in practice. We love to encourage people to embrace their entrepreneurial spirit and pursue their passions. *Be your own boss. Build your own company.* But that liberating Jerry Maguire moment is never where the story ends.

"I'm pretty restless, and I think I don't deal well with authority figures for long periods of time," Eli said. "But with freelancing, it's so easy because it's all short term. I just have to keep them happy enough so they hire me again. I don't have to kiss ass every fucking day. I like having a mixture of being home and being out in other places. I don't always want to go into an office. I want to have some days where I can do whatever I feel like doing at my own pace. Sometimes I want to be around people and have some structure. And then that gets old. Everything gets old."

Unlike back when he was trekking around Brooklyn filming bands, most of Eli's days are spent editing. He's learned over time that editing is his particular strength.

"I'm a good shooter, but I'm not like, 'Okay, we need this lens for this scene.' I can't do the lighting ratio math in my head. I don't want to have to haul camera shit all over the place. I'm too old for it. My back isn't good. Years of just standing with cameras has messed me up."

"Did you always know you wanted to end up doing something in the arts?" I asked.

"I did," he said. "I was grandiose in my early twenties. I wanted to make something great, but I didn't know what it was. So I didn't know what medium I would end up trying to do that in. It was hard for me to admit to myself that I was very good at wanting to be great, but I didn't know how to pursue it. I hit a ceiling with drawing. I hit a ceiling with guitar, which I took up seriously when I was recording bands. I thought I wanted to be a musician. I was practicing, like, six hours a day at one point, but I realized I didn't want to perform."

"And with shooting and editing you never hit that kind of ceiling where you wanted to quit?" I said.

"Yeah. Being behind the camera was a really comfortable place for me. That's where I started—with that idea. Working at Pitchfork was like getting paid to go to film school. It was great. I had no formal training. I dove in. I was like, 'I *have* to figure this out.' I really liked telling stories, and this was a medium where I could do that and it fit my personality."

Eli's artistic path had taken him from comic book artist to waiter to paralegal to almost law student to art gallery assistant to guitar player to recorder of bands to staff video editor/producer/director at a major music website to freelance video editor/director working for himself. It had been a winding journey, and he hadn't any clue in the midst of it that he would end up where he was now.

Artistic callings in particular are "supposed" to hit early and enduringly, but for many of us, what hits early is the desire to express something, to "make something great." We wind our way, sometimes very slowly, toward a creative medium in which we have talent, yes, but maybe even more important, I realized from talking to Eli, we need to find one aligned with our temperament.

On Being Suited to Your Calling

If Eli had persevered with drawing, his first passion, he would never have found his way to this alignment. The same is true with Sarah and the flute. In fact, Eli had to quit a bunch of things before he found a creative career that stuck. He had what some psychologists would call a growth versus a fixed mind-set. He cultivated passion instead of simply waiting for one to find him. "People are often told to find their passion, as though passions and interests are pre-formed and must simply be discovered . . ." as three researchers recently put it in the journal *Psychological Science*. "Urging people to find their passion may lead them to put all their eggs in one basket but then to drop that basket when it becomes difficult to carry." The researchers found that those with a more flexible mind-set had advantages in motivation and persistence when exploring new interests. And part of pursuing new interests and seeing what sticks is a process of figuring out what kind of person you are. It takes time to learn how your personality aligns with your passion. (Though I feel compelled to note that *growth mind-set*, like *grit*, has become yet another oversimplified self-esteem buzzword we've indiscriminately applied in educational settings where there are far more variables for success than simply believing in yourself.)

Sure, scientists have noted that creative people have certain personality traits in common, things like openness to experience, tolerance for ambiguity, curiosity, intrinsic motivation, and trust in intuition. But even these general traits play out differently in each person. Eli is an artistic person, but he had to find the right fit for his unique artistic personality. There is no one size that fits all. To know where to put your energies, you must get to know yourself.

After my conversation with Eli, I started noticing examples of successful creative people who have talked or written about transitioning from one creative medium to another. The actress Parker Posey used to be a ballerina, for example. The North Carolina School of the Arts rejected her as a teen when she applied to their dance program. When her dad called to ask what he should tell his heartbroken daughter, the dean of the school said, "Tell her she's an actress." The writer Meghan Daum has written about being a childhood musician; so has the writer Dani Shapiro, who played the piano. The actor Zach Woods from *The Office* and *Silicon Valley* was a serious trumpet player growing up. When the comedian Marc Maron interviewed him, Woods joked about how part of committing to his identity as a jazz musician meant wearing a fedora for most of seventh and eighth grades. But then there was a moment in the conversation when Woods got serious. He spoke about how disappointed he felt years after quitting when he picked up his instrument to try to play: "I was really upset. It doesn't hold up well to neglect." They stick with us, those early identities and pursuits, even when we let them go, even when we are successful in another endeavor.

Very few of us know exactly what we want to do from an

early age and end up doing it in exactly the way we imagined. I thought of Ben Foster as one of those kinds of people, but really I had no idea. I hadn't spoken to him in over two decades and had no clue if he saw his own narrative as the same straight line as I did.

Eli's strengths were that he experimented and worked hard each time he tried something new. He knew he wanted to be creative in his career, but he didn't hold himself to a particular type of artistic identity or field. He let himself explore and make mistakes along the way.

During all the earlier moments I had examined my path from music to writing, I had never given being suited to one's calling the attention it deserved. We're taught that personality, like socioeconomics and talent, is a variable of success we can control.

But being a writer suited my unhacked personality more than music ever had—its day-to-day rhythms and particular brand of solitude and flow. Also, like Eli, I was more comfortable behind the scenes. I did miss performing, but by the time I got to college, my anxiety about it was unmanageable for someone who intended to be onstage for a living. I was on a ski team when I was little. I loved the speed and adrenaline of racing. Until one day shortly after puberty hit, when suddenly I didn't. Instead of excitement, I felt dread. Instead of freedom, I felt fear. Fear is another thing we're supposed to fight through. You can fight mental fear on a lot of fronts, but once fear settles into the body, well, that's a different story. You'll miscalculate the zig, lose your footing on the zag. You won't go as fast or as hard, and you've got to go fast and hard in a race. I kept skiing after I realized the bodily fear wasn't going anywhere, but I did stop racing. Don't worry. This was no great loss to the sport of skiing. That same kind of bodily fear did a number on me in college. I lost my confidence. We could argue all day about whether I should have tried harder to hack my fear and keep playing viola, but it's another question altogether if it would have aligned with my personality to do so.

In addition, the desire to perform is not the same as the desire to practice. That's an obvious point, but one I failed to grasp for a long time. Writing was different. I loved the practice part of it. Yes, I would *also* love to be a celebrated author, but when I asked myself if I'd give up writing, even if I never got my writer's fantasy life, the answer was an easy no.

I need writing more than I needed the viola. I know this because it stuck and music didn't. The pressure and competition of music ruined it for me. This wasn't true with writing. Even though my fantasy of the writer's life has dissipated, my desire to keep writing remains intact. At the same time—and this counterintuitive distinction is difficult to articulate—while I need writing more than music, I think I might love it slightly less, and that this is a good thing for me in terms of enduring. Writing doesn't break my heart the same way music did. Playing viola was so visceral and physical. I'm more in my head as a writer and less in my body. And something about that difference allows me to have some constructive distance from it and makes the frustrations a little easier to tolerate.

What I'd come to realize I wasn't suited to, however, was

my fantasy of the free-spirited freelance writer in that Lower East Side loft. I'd had my managing editor job for almost a year. I'd promised myself at the year mark I'd go back to the freelancer grind, but every time I really considered quitting, a screenshot of my reliable direct-deposited paycheck popped into my head. Yes, I had slightly less time for writing, but that time was being used to work on pieces I really wanted to write as opposed to saying yes to everything that came my way.

For Eli, saying yes to everything was worth it, even if it meant prioritizing paying projects over his own, because the day-to-day rhythms of freelancing suited his personality. He wasn't free to choose his own projects, but he was free to do them on his own time. I didn't want to write about heat-resistant makeup or make lists of the best beaches. I so very much did not want to write about those things that taking another job to pay my rent was preferable. Simple as that. Well, complicated as that, because accepting this meant being very specific about what kind of negotiated freedom was most important to me instead of adhering to some romanticized idea of it.

"Do what you love" is such dangerously vague advice. It's how your love manifests itself that will tell you if you should try making a living from it. We put so much pressure on passion, but that's just a jumping-off point. I was a fragile musician, and fragile things understandably break. Knowing and accepting that meant I could better appreciate the fact that when music dropped away, it made room for writing to take its place.

On Remembering Something Simple and True About Success

I asked Eli the question I eventually got around to asking all my old friends: Do you think you fulfilled your potential?

"Oh, I don't know. I guess so." He laughed. "I haven't done everything I want to do—that's for sure—creatively I've not done it yet . . . but I feel like I was never good at putting myself in a good position to get what I wanted. I always just flailed around and figured things out. But suddenly I'm like, 'I sort of see how in the future I could build on things I'm doing now.' That's a really new feeling for me. So maybe things are going okay."

Eli hadn't had an aha moment. Instead, over time, and by being flexible, including being willing to quit things when he hit a ceiling, he found an alignment between his calling and his personality. We love to focus on how hard something is we're trying to achieve. We see adversity as sweetening our ultimate success. Yes, sure, but we should also take note of what feels "easy." That's a sign, too. Hard work is vital, but there is also a sense of ease (not easiness, but inner ease, similar to the way Eli talked about not hitting a ceiling) that comes when we find this alignment.

For the most part, we're all just figuring things out, of course, to greater or lesser degrees. Some of us stop flailing at three and some of us at thirty-three and some of us at seventy-three. Some of us find our passions early on, like Jenna, and some of us take much longer. And some people never find a work passion and put their passion elsewhere. This is good, too.

"You seem pretty relaxed about figuring it out as you go versus having some master plan," I said.

"When I was working at Pitchfork, I was dealing with a lot of kids who were, like, twenty years old who hit the lottery with their shitty band. They weren't going to succeed beyond one album, and then the fame went away. These kids were in this weird place. A lot of them didn't understand what was going on, and I could see that. At the same time I also felt like, 'Man, that was so easy for them to get that success.' But I feel like there's a slow burn for most people, and then one day you're in your fifties and you're really running shit. Who wouldn't love it to happen earlier?"

A slow burn. I liked that. I'd always been obsessed with the fast burn, with not only achievement but precocious achievement. We celebrate prodigies bursting onto the scene and venerate old masters with lifetime achievement awards. Being somewhere between beginner and seasoned professional is a trickier place. Have you ever decided to swim out to a buoy and realized halfway there that the distance was way farther than it looked from the shore? You feel good, strong, and powerful, but this doesn't make that distance any less daunting. The middle feels like that sometimes, at least to me. But maybe there is also something freeing about aging out of the period of potential precociousness. Now instead of envying those on the "20 Under 35" list, you can focus that energy instead on your work. Besides, progress is incremental for most of us. It takes time to figure out who we are and what we want.

"What's your definition of success?" I asked Eli.

"Well, it would be doing good work, getting paid enough to live, and to save some money. You know, of course who doesn't want to win an Oscar, but that's lottery shit. The only thing you can do is do good work. And then at least you're playing the lottery. You have a chance. I'd be happy just to be a reasonably successful workaday editor, but I'd love it if I got to a point where people liked seeing the stuff I make and were like, 'Make more.'"

"That's the dream, people waiting for your next thing," I said.

"That would be amazing," Eli said. His cat jumped up onto the couch and nudged his hand. Eli absent-mindedly stroked her white fur and didn't say anything for a few seconds.

"But the fact that I'm making money doing something I like at *all* considering how many jobs I had where I hated everything about them and wasn't making very much money . . . In a lot of ways, that is enough. I still have hints of that grandiose impulse. *You gotta make something great.* I'm still working on that, because I haven't made anything great yet. When I do, I'll hopefully feel even better about things. But I feel great about just the fact that I can pay my rent making videos."

I resolved in that moment to hold on to this slippery truth I had the habit of forgetting: how lucky I am to take any pleasure *at all* in my work. "Writing is hard . . . ," writes

Cheryl Strayed. "Coal mining is harder. Do you think miners stand around all day talking about how hard it is to mine for coal? They do not. They simply *dig*."

ELI LIVES IN BUSHWICK, Brooklyn. I went to visit him a few weeks after our dinner, walking from the subway past an old auto repair shop. A heavily tattooed worker in overalls was smoking out front. A few doors down, I passed a new hip café where twentysomethings with headphones were tapping away on computers. The facades of nearly every building in the three-block stretch from the subway to Eli's place were covered in graffiti. A small group of tourists was ambling along snapping photos of the colorful murals from every available angle. This combination of grit and gentrification was Bushwick 2015 in a nutshell, a neighborhood in an interesting liminal space, including when it came to its artist residents.

It had become a definitive hub for artists, as affordable studio space had shifted over the decades from Manhattan's West Side to the Lower East Side to Williamsburg to Bushwick. As I write this, there are over sixty galleries in the 1.3-square-mile neighborhood. A yearly Bushwick Open Studios event was just starting to draw crowds around the time I visited Eli and is now a major community event.

Eli moved here in 2009, six years before *Vogue* named it one of the "coolest" neighborhoods in the world. He liked the neighborhood more before it was the "epicenter of hip shit," but he felt like it was still a good place for creative people. Besides, his big one-bedroom was rent-stabilized, and for an artist it doesn't get any better than that. He shared it with his girlfriend of seven years, a photo editor at *The New York Times* who worked the night shift.

In a small alcove office, the psychedelic screen saver on Eli's giant Mac glowed. He pointed out three stacked cardboard boxes where he kept his childhood comics organized in protective plastic covers.

"I have all the individual comics stored in these boxes and all the compendiums on those bookshelves. And my graphic novels."

"What are you going to do with them?" I said.

"I just like them. I think they are great artifacts. I imagine that if I have kids, they are going to be interested in them, but I'm also going to be like, 'Yo, you gotta be careful with them, don't bend the spines!'" He laughed.

I thought of my viola back in my bedroom. I felt this pressure to play it—it was there to be played, wasn't it? And if not, shouldn't I be practical and sell it? It's not like I couldn't use the money. But Eli wasn't selling his comics. He liked having them around. He liked the idea of passing them on one day. It seems so silly that I didn't realize this was a perfectly acceptable framing for my relationship to my instrument. To say: I don't actively need this viola anymore, but I don't want to get rid of it, either. It reminds me of a time and a place and a part of myself. And that's enough, at least for now.

I asked Eli if he had a sense of where he wanted to be professionally in five or ten years.

"I have a sense," he said. He told me about a friend of his who had just turned forty. "He's a really, really good editor. He cut a critically acclaimed music documentary recently. He does legit stuff. People pitch him to come cut their project. He's super serious about being an editor and less concerned about making his own movies. Part of me thinks that maybe I should just go down that road, but I also love shooting my own stuff. I've been working on all these short-form things for the last two years, and I think the time has come where I really need to figure out a bigger topic I can make a full-length film about. I want something of mine on Netflix or somewhere similar. That would be awesome."

I don't think Eli saying he has a sense of where he wants to be implies he isn't as hungry or strategic as the next guy. Or, I don't know, maybe it does. But what it *does* indicate to me is that he is adaptable and flexible, and those traits have definitely served him well.

6

Never Compromise!
(But Definitely Compromise)

I was headed to L.A. for the Oscars. No, I wasn't going to be dressed by Carolina Herrera or given a goodie bag worth thousands of dollars at the end of the evening, but this trip was the closest I might ever get. In a plot twist I definitely didn't see coming, I had started dating one of Adam's best friends. The buzz around that screenplay written by Adam's former writing partner had bloomed into an actual Oscar nomination—and we were going to California to cheer him on.

Someone our age has been nominated for a goddamn Oscar, I thought to myself as we drove away from the airport. A writer, no less. He now owned a beautiful house on a hill. His deck overlooked a smattering of much smaller homes I imagined populated by not-Oscar-nominated screenwriters. A bunch of us were going to watch the awards show from his living room while he schmoozed in person with Hollywood stars he now counted as friends. I was a little jealous of it all: the success, the house, the glamour. How could one not be?

We opened bottle after bottle of wine and poured pop-corn into bowls. Somebody ordered a bunch of pizzas. When the Best Adapted Screenplay category was announced, the room went silent. They called five names, showed five film clips, and then . . . he WON. Everyone in the room screamed and high-fived and hugged. We watched in awe as he accepted his golden statue and delivered a moving acceptance speech.

Adam understandably looked a bit stunned. I wanted to ask him what he was feeling, but I held back. We were walking a fine line these days. We had become close since I started dating his friend. We saw each other fairly often and talked openly about our personal and professional lives—but he of course knew I was working on a book that he would appear in, and he was careful about what he did and didn't say to me.

In the months since Adam and I had reconnected, his ex–writing partner had been showered with public recognition for his movie. He was constantly traveling and giving talks; he had just signed a book contract for a novel and was writing a screenplay with major stars already attached to it. And now an *Oscar*. It must have been a lot to absorb, even for someone as grounded as Adam.

Later that night, once everyone else had gone home, Adam did offer up a brief summary of what he thought this moment meant for his friend: "He'll be able to work on whatever he wants for the rest of his life. For the rest of his life, his name will be preceded by *Oscar winner*."

THE NEXT MORNING I got to snap some selfies with the Oscar. I texted them to my film professor dad.

"Wow! It's almost like *you* won an Oscar!" he texted back.

My dad's enthusiasm was cute—he's always been my biggest cheerleader. Obviously, this was *nothing* like my almost winning an Oscar, but that's the thing about standing so close to someone else's success. It feels within reach. One big hit. One smart choice. One stroke of luck. That could be you, with your house on the hill and your million-dollar view, getting to work on whatever you want for the rest of your life.

The Fulfilled Creative Director

The day after the Oscars I hopped into a rental car to go interview my camp crush, Daniel, who also lived in L.A. Adam and Daniel had both grown up in Chicago and had friends in common, so they occasionally ran into each other.

"He's a nice, nice guy," Adam said when I told him I was headed out to see Daniel. Ever the archive of preteen memories, he added: "I remember at camp girls used to say, 'He has such hairy legs!' That was a thing girls said to mean he was manly."

"He *was* manly," I said.

"Oh, jeez," Adam said, rolling his eyes.

Daniel was the prototype of the artsy, aloof, long-haired Jordan Catalano–type guy I crushed hard on throughout my teens and early twenties. When we had spoken on the phone a few weeks earlier, I had fully regressed to my nervous twelve-year-old self, fumbling like an idiot through questions. *What do you do on, like, a typical day at your job? Was there a lot of pressure on you to succeed, or whatever? Have you given any thought to the idea that we should totally have ended up together as, like, a couple?* (I didn't really ask that last question. Come on, guys. I'm a professional.)

Similar to sentiments expressed by all my old friends, Daniel remembered camp as "a place where people got me." It was also where he decided he wanted to be an actor after seeing his twelve-year-old bunkmate in a play. That bunkmate? Ben Foster, of course.

"He was in a play called *Juvie*. He played a meth addict. It was the first time I'd seen someone act in something where I was like, 'That isn't someone I know, that's someone else.' That was the moment. I wanted to do *that*."

He wasn't the first or the last person I interviewed to mention Ben's performance in *Juvie*. It seemed legendary among the actor kids, imprinted as the first time many of them took serious stock of their own talent. It was one of those pivotal moments in which a kid might either recognize the limits of her own ability and choose another path or, as was the case with Daniel, double down on his dream. Ben's talent was so proximal to Daniel—literally in the same bunk bed—that I wondered if it felt kind of like when I held that Oscar.

Interlochen was also where Daniel learned that being creative could be a career. Neither of his parents was in the arts, and back home he was a popular jock. His artistic side wasn't a secret, nor was he self-conscious about it; it just wasn't cultivated in any real way until Interlochen. Getting to go somewhere you could be creative and have other people be interested in what you were doing, where you were rewarded for trying something new, and where, unlike Daniel's later experience as a screenwriter in Hollywood, you didn't have to be guarded about your ideas—well, he said, "It was like Hogwarts for artistic kids."

His reference to this magical world felt particularly apt when I found out Daniel currently worked as a creative director at a massive visual effects studio. Like Adam, despite his early kid ambitions, he had transitioned from acting to screenwriting. He applied to the University of Southern California, knowing it was a stretch school but telling himself that if he didn't get in, it was a sign he should pursue something else instead. He got accepted, and in film school he sold a screenplay. He was only twenty-one and thought it was his big break.

"I thought: This will get made into a movie and I'll go see it!" he told me. "I couldn't even imagine a scenario where someone would buy something and not make it, but that's what happened." (Fun fact: an unproduced screenplay has about a 0.3 percent chance of being made into a feature film.)

"And then I wrote a concept for a reality show. I thought, *Okay, this costs nothing to make. It will air quickly.* It ended up being three years of back and forth. I remember sitting in a meeting and thinking that if we put all the money we had paid execs and lawyers into this, we could have made it by now."

Daniel's career as a screenwriter had been feast or famine. He'd make good money selling something but then run out of it by the time he sold the next thing. He loved writing but realized over time that he hated the business of being a screenwriter. He wanted to work on something that more than just a few execs in a room ever saw, and he wanted to get back to some of his visual arts roots—which was how he ended up in a trainee program at the visual effects company where he's now on staff. This was during one of his famine periods.

"Prior to this job I would write screenplays until I was out of money and then go and get a job on a commercial or video game set," he said. "I came here to learn special effects because I thought it would be another skill for one of those side gigs. And then I'd go sell another script and go back to screenwriting, the way I'd been doing it—back and forth, back and forth. But I ended up enjoying it here so much. I was being paid to write but also to be creative in other ways."

Daniel was kind of the anti-Eli, at least at the moment in their lives when I caught up with them. Whereas Eli prized the day-to-day freedom of his work life above all else, Daniel's priority was seeing projects he worked on get made, and showing up to an office every day was how he could make that happen.

"Five or six years ago, when I was writing full time, I never thought I'd work in an office," he said. "But this job blends everything I wanted to do in my career: writing, directing, visual arts. It's so much more interesting than sitting around in my apartment."

Daniel was waiting in the lobby when I arrived. While still cute, he was more Ben Affleck now than Jordan Catalano, with short hair and a trim beard. He led the way to a screening room where his colleague, Alice, was pulling up some footage of their latest project. Alice emanated the earnest enthusiasm of someone who really enjoys her work. When I asked Daniel to describe his job to me in layman's terms, she chimed in, almost bouncing out of her seat: "We make magic!"

Daniel and Alice worked mostly on commercials and video games. They had recently done Super Bowl promos for *Heroes Reborn*, a television event miniseries, and were currently working on a commercial for Charles Schwab. The company was launching an online investment program and pivoting from their typical "Chuck talks to the viewer" ad campaigns to ones where a futuristic-looking computer would address potential clients. Daniel was the creative director on the visual side, a role in which he was both creatively involved in the project, designing the visual elements of the commercial, and the business-minded exec who sat with the client to convince them to buy into his company's vision for the ad.

"The things that get the most attention are weird or beautiful or funny," he said. "At the same time, your client doesn't want to feel like they are throwing their money away, so you have to couch it in terms of something that already works. I'm consistently intrigued by that challenge. The best way to handle it is learning what people want and then giving them the best version of what they think they want. You twist what they want."

Daniel's job also required him to figure out how to balance what the client requested with what could realistically be done given the budget and time frame, and he had discovered that he liked navigating that type of creative/business challenge, too.

Daniel and Alice played me what they had so far. The commercial was in what's called the previsualization (previs) stage of the process. The opening shot was of a blue computer in a sterile gray room. As the camera panned, Alfred Molina's soothing English accent told me how I could intelligently invest.

"The process for this commercial has been very iterative," he said. "They literally didn't know what they wanted the computer to look like. When we first heard about the job, we were like, 'It's just a box in a room? How will you make one commercial, let alone six commercials?' It remains to be seen how the audiences will react to it."

Unlike when Daniel was a screenwriter, the projects he works on here almost always get made and seen by way more people than a few execs in a room. And he doesn't have to wait months or years for his ideas to come to life.

"A video game trailer I write will have a whole team of

artists animating it. It's amazing that you can get an idea and communicate it and a day later it's there. It's not an idea on paper. It's an actual thing in a 3-D space in the world. That's really rewarding."

The company he works for is one of the largest, most innovative visual effects companies in the world. In addition to the commercials and video games Daniel works on, they also do visual effects for feature films.

"I can't tell you everything we're working on, but *Fast & Furious* we can talk about because the companies doing special effects got announced when they pushed the film back. For features, we're normally under super tight non-disclosure agreements."

"Why do you need NDAs for special effects?" I said.

"Partly it's data security," Daniel said. "We have all this crazy security stuff because they don't want anything from our computers to be able to leak out of the building. Our computers don't have USB ports. But partly it's because certain types of films don't want to draw attention to their special effects. For some movies, the magic is meant to be invisible."

"There are two types of visual effects," Alice said. "You can do a movie like *Tron* with tons of obvious visual effects, but a movie like *Furious 7*, well, those you don't want people to notice."

"Obviously everyone knows someone is going to do stuff with Paul Walker," Daniel said. (The actor died in a car accident while they were filming.) "But if you saw other parts of the movie the artists are working on you'd be like, 'Wow, I had no idea that's visual effects.' We have dozens of artists working on stuff that would just be invisible to you."

Alice said that when she goes to movies now she can't help pointing out effects to other people. "I'm like, 'That's not real, that's not real, that's not real,'" she said.

"What's an example of a recent movie that you wouldn't guess has special effects?" I asked.

"*Gone Girl*," Alice said.

"*Gone Girl*?" I said. "Huh."

"The snow," she said.

"Yeah," Daniel said. "Both of the scenes where he touches her lips. The snow's not real."

"They wanted you to make snow instead of having somebody just drop it?" I asked.

"It's faster," Daniel explained. "Time is the most valuable commodity on the feature side. Let's say in the old days, we're talking like ten years ago, if you were firing a gun into a wall, you'd put little explosive things into the wall and they'd pop out. Now you'd never do that. It takes a lot of time to rig, and if you mess up the scene, you have to go back and redo the wall and everyone is standing around waiting for you. So now that will all just be CG."

The company has a whole library of elements that include common effects like a gun being fired into a wall. They can slow down the footage and pull out elements like debris or sparks flying from the gun after it goes off.

"We're starting to get more into water," Alice said. "Water is really difficult. In the old days they would make physical models and put them in a bathtub and shoot it. And then they'd put little people on them. Now we make CG models and we make CG water."

They told me the "water guys" were the cream of the crop in terms of visual effects. Well, them and the "dust guys."

"Fire is also hard," Daniel said. "And hair. The more natural a thing is, the more elemental, the harder it is to make. Because the harder it is to trick our eye into believing it's normal."

It's only recently that artists started going to school specifically for visual effects. Everyone Daniel's age and older has a background like his—some screenwriting, some time in the commercial industry, a talent for visual arts, a few years of working on and off on film sets. Daniel wound up in a job he'd never imagined for himself, one that hadn't even existed when we were kids at Interlochen. As was true with Eli, it had taken him a while to figure out in what way he would make a living being creative. He'd had to acknowledge that his idea of being a screenwriter didn't match the reality of the endeavor, and he'd had to be open to new outlets for his talent.

When I arrived, Daniel had walked me past two cavernous rooms where hundreds of computer artists sat at any given time. He couldn't take me inside because of the NDAs, but he said that if he could, I would see row upon row of screens with beautiful images being manipulated.

"A lot of people have tried to say what they are doing isn't art, but it *is*," he said.

I had a feeling that broadening his notion of being an artist had been part of Daniel's path, too. He struck me as someone who saw creativity as an expansive idea, not a narrow one, one that could incorporate everything from creative problem-solving for a client to creativity on a computer screen.

WE SAID GOODBYE to Alice so Daniel could take me on a tour of the rest of the building. Posters of films his company has worked on lined the hallways: *The Curious Case of Benjamin Button, The Fifth Element, Her, Fight Club.* We walked toward a six-foot statue of a woman in a tank top and cargo pants whose bust-to-hip ratio would have made Barbie blush.

"Angelina Jolie as Lara Croft?" I guessed.

"She did the movie, but this is from the video game," Daniel said. "This is one of the products we wrote and created the entire campaign for. We came up with an idea of Lara in the second game dealing with PTSD from the first game. The client said, 'As long as you show her also kicking ass, we think it's awesome.' The story line got a lot of attention. People were like, 'Oh, you guys are finally taking responsibility for the heroine of your piece.' And we're like, '*Yes,* that's what we're doing.' The client sent us this as a thank-you. They didn't tell us what it was when they sent it. This giant box just showed up, and there she was."

Here was another interesting plot twist I'd never thought much about. For some people, like Daniel, what you once envisioned as your paycheck-driven (and often team-oriented) day job ends up having a bigger impact, creative or otherwise, than your passion-driven individual creative work. The literary agent writing her novel on the side spends her career helping other people get published. The producer working on his own songs gets someone else to the top of the charts along the way. The creative director who writes screenplays ends up changing the cultural dialogue about video-game heroines through writing dialogue for someone else's creation.

I'd been feeling this with my own day job the longer I was there—how even though I called my writing my "real work," I took a fair amount of pride in being part of a team who helped publish research that shaped policies and programs around the world.

"That's so cool," I said, and I meant it. I'm embarrassed to say that before we talked, I didn't really believe Daniel could be happier doing this than working on his own screenplays. I could see now that it was another way in which my relationship with creativity was too limited. I had limited it with ideas about ownership and credit, whereas Daniel thrived in this collaborative environment where he and his team worked together to bring something to life.

"Do you feel creatively fulfilled here?" I asked Daniel, though the answer seemed obvious, given everything he'd said so far.

"It's super rewarding," he said. "It takes all your attention. I'll sometimes realize I've gone a month without writing my own stuff and I didn't notice it because I've been so busy working on other things here that are so interesting.

Right now I'm working on the opening title sequence for a movie. It's a big horror action movie that requires a lot of background. We've watched the early clips, and there's a lot of exposition that they don't cover in the movie. They came to us and said, 'Can you create something that shows the world of the movie and also explains certain ideas?' It's fun because I'm getting to write dialogue for this big block-buster movie. The idea that you can communicate this idea to somebody and then a few days later you see it, it's magical that way."

"When we spoke on the phone, you talked about being frustrated earlier in your career by how someone could buy a script of yours and then it never got made," I said.

"Yeah, for me that's the biggest difference between working here and working as a screenwriter. I really was sick of not seeing the things that I had written get made. I got into the mode of thinking of the script I was writing as an actual thing, which is a dangerous mode for screenwriters in particular. You're writing a movie; you're not writing a script. Any other kind of writer can say, *I'm writing a novel.* You can read the novel. But screenwriting is more like architectural blueprints. No architect would ever say, *Hey, look at these blueprints I drew.* Screenwriting is one of the only industries where people are like, 'Look at this blueprint of this thing no one ever built!'"

His comment reminded me of how Eli hit all those ceilings before he settled into his current creative profession, how Sarah had realized she didn't actually want the type of musician's life on offer in New York, how I had realized that being a freelance writer was actually a lot less free than I had imagined. Like the rest of us, Daniel had to experience the nitty-gritty of his dream job before he could adjust his life/career plan accordingly.

"Are you still working on your own screenplays?" I asked Daniel.

"Yes, I'm trying. There is a great J. K. Rowling quote: 'Every minute I took to write *Harry Potter* was a minute stolen from something else.' I might be butchering that. I very much feel that way about screenwriting. You must feel that, too. You told me on the phone you had recently taken a part-time job."

"It's actually been almost a year," I said, realizing that saying *recently* was no longer accurate. "I'd gotten really tired of the constant hustle and having to say yes to everything. Now I publish less than I used to, but I get to work on more of what I actually want to write. I'm still trying to find a balance."

It was the first time I'd acknowledged out loud my own artistic compromise and the reasons I'd made it. Just as Daniel had figured out that he prized above all else seeing stuff he worked on get made, I had realized that what mattered to me most was choosing my writing projects, even if that meant finding other (or additional) ways to make money.

"It's funny that you say that," Daniel said. "Earlier in the week I had lunch with a friend. This was the whole subject of our conversation. How do you balance? In my twenties I thought I did it really well, and it's only now I think, *Oh, I could have had a different kind of balance that whole time.*"

On Compromise and Longing

Daniel's path was the slippery slope into office life I'd once feared, where you wake up one day and realize you haven't worked on your own writing for a month. But his enthusiasm for his cool job made it obvious that what I had initially interpreted as a compromise of his creative dreams was actually the fulfillment of what he had realized was most important to him: getting his work made and seen. In the end, it all came back to one's individually calibrated version of balance.

My job as the managing editor of an academic journal wasn't the same as Daniel's gig. It mostly wasn't creative, but it also wasn't mindless or physically exhausting like the waitressing/bartending jobs I'd had over the years, or as off-hours time-consuming as grading and class prep had been when I was an adjunct lecturer. It left me plenty of mental space and free time to write, and to write without constantly worrying about how to make a living.

Having money isn't supposed to matter to an artist, but this is just more art monster mythology that discourages aspiring creatives. Michelangelo played the part of the starving artist but had plenty of cash. Everyone remembers the "room of one's own" part of Virginia Woolf's famous essay, but her thesis is that "a woman must have money and a room of her own if she is to write fiction." *Money.* Even the Bohemians thought that by thirty you should no longer be starving.

Everyone has to make her own call about how much financial insecurity she can handle. Eli, for example, compared his overall annual freelance income to his former full-time wage and simply made it work. But for me, the unpredictability of when and how much I would make every month was what I had despised as a freelancer. I couldn't budget for anything because I never knew how much money I was going to have at any given time.

Being a managing editor also fed the practical, organized side of my personality that I often downplayed in favor of my creative side. My role was essentially that of a project manager—corralling the various players involved in bringing a scholarly journal to life (authors, editors, production team, publisher). And it was, dare I confess it, kind of *nice* to have some of my days devoted to checking tasks off a list instead of staring down at a blank page. That was another kind of balance that I had to figure out worked for me: having part of my week be creative and spontaneous and another part be practical and organized. "I had erred not only in my prediction of who I would become, but also in my understanding of who I was," writes Jesse Browner in his memoir *How Did I Get Here? Making Peace with the Road Not Taken.*

I had less time to write now, but the time I did have felt less frenetic: my mind wasn't racing through pitches or spent frantically scribbling my monthly budget on a scrap piece of paper. Staying at the journal was not a matter of accepting canned clichés about whether real artists have day jobs, another seductive art monster cliché. When I think about this,

I always hear Picasso and Oscar Wilde in a fake debate in my head, Picasso screaming, "The 'second career' is an illusion!" while Wilde calmly counters that "the best work in literature is always done by those who do not depend on it for their daily bread." That's the thing about quotes. You can always find one to support whatever you've already made up your mind about or to make you feel bad about.

No, appreciating my day job was about accepting that I personally was someone who needed more financial stability than I had previously imagined. It was about the fact that I didn't want to constantly hustle, pitch, and attend PR events where I had to pretend to care about Montreal's 375th anniversary (no offense, Montreal!) just so I could say I made my living as a writer. As Jesse Browner notes, writers "are faced with a stark, simple choice: either we set out to make our living by our pen, by writing what we know will sell enough to feed, clothe, and house us and our families, or we write precisely what suits us and stop complaining about how we have to find alternate income."

For many of us, there inevitably will be compromises like day jobs. I think we can more easily value those compromises by clearly defining for ourselves not only what they take away but also what they offer—if we see these choices as aligned with the hard-earned wisdom of what we really value in our creative lives as opposed to what we've been told about artistic success.

Of course, there is still the question of longing. Yes, after talking to Daniel, I had a newfound appreciation for my day job. Did that mean a part of me didn't also fantasize about that lightning-strike moment when something I had written—something that came unasked for out of my heart and mind and mouth and gut, to paraphrase the brilliant drunk Charles Bukowski—also turned out to be a huge critical success and I didn't need to have any job at all other than writing, reading, and thinking at my leisure? Of course not.

We're not supposed to long for things. We're supposed to act to get what we want, and longing is seen as inaction. Longing is complacency. Longing is refusing to be grateful for (and upbeat about) what you have. Longing is misplaced nostalgia. It is true that an overindulgence in longing can ruin the present moment. "Do not spoil what you have by desiring what you have not; but remember that what you now have was once among things only hoped for," wrote the wise Epicurus. But some longing is natural, isn't it?

Jesse Browner's memoir led me back to the work of psychoanalyst/essayist Adam Phillips. In *Missing Out: In Praise of the Unlived Life*, Phillips writes (by way of Camus) about how the gap between what we want and what we have is "our link, our connection, to the world." You cannot have satisfaction without frustration, Phillips argues. Experiencing the former requires experiencing the latter because we define the feelings in contrast to one another: "If this was quantifiable we would say that the good life proposed by psychoanalysis is one in which there is just the right amount of frustration . . . But it seems as though it is all the wrong kinds of frustration that make our lives what they are; that so much depends on what each of us makes of the too much and the too little we get."

We see compromise as antithetical to success because we believe it means that we didn't get what we wanted, and not getting what we want is by default a bad thing. So the idea of some amount of frustration being not just acceptable but *desirable* was novel to me. It meant that it was okay that I might forever be evaluating my various compromises, that I didn't have to hope to reach a higher spiritual plane where I was totally free from the suffering of self-doubt, uncertainty, and what-ifs. It meant compromise was not a solid state; it was constant liquid negotiation.

Rebecca Solnit's *A Field Guide to Getting Lost* offered me another version of the idea that it is okay to long for things, that we should accept our inevitable ongoing longing instead of treating it like a problem that requires fixing: "for something of this longing will, like the blue of distance, only be relocated, not assuaged, by acquisition and arrival, just as the mountains cease to be blue when you arrive among them and the blue instead tints the next beyond."

We are told to act when we are frustrated. Action is good—you don't want to needlessly long for things within reach—but as someone who can be relentlessly action-oriented, I found the simple psychic acknowledgment that longing is normal such a relief. We don't need to cure frustration and longing, because these feelings are a fundamental part of being human.

We can value the compromises we make while also leaning into the "texture of longing" in our lives. In other words, we are capable of and allowed to have mixed fucking feelings about things.

I decided to write Jesse Browner, the author of that memoir I've been quoting. We worked a few blocks from each other (I knew this from the book, not because I am a stalker). I asked if he would be willing to meet for coffee. I ostensibly wanted to talk about his book, but I also just wanted advice—advice about living in New York, about that slippery slope into office life, about the logistics of balancing work and relationships. He had become a kind of mentor to me through his book. At the same time, I felt a similar skepticism as when I talked with Jenna. Sure, he'd written a book about finding contentment and balance as a writer with a day job, but if I stared into his soul over coffee, would I see someone who was really and truly satisfied?

"I was surprised to get an email from someone your age," he said when we met at Le Pain Quotidien one morning. You won't be surprised given my obsession with potential that this made me feel weirdly proud of my precocious midlife crisis.

He had nothing but kind things to say. About my job: "That's a great gig for a writer." About the pressure of finishing the book: "Even when you're not working, you're working. Go easy on yourself." I tried in my not-subtle way to root out if he was genuinely content with his day job/ writing balance.

"The only regret I have is wishing I'd reconciled myself to the job earlier," he told me.

Phillips writes that the point of learning from experience is "finding ways of making your needs compatible with living in the world." That process takes as long as it takes. Hopefully not a lifetime.

I thought of how when I asked Jenna about touring with Arcade Fire, she said that maybe she'd go, but that she didn't pine for that opportunity. I thought of Daniel stealing time for his screenplay but happy with the collaborative creative work that took up most of his week. If I could be a full-time writer working on exactly what I wanted without ever worrying about money, would I? Absolutely. But that's lottery shit, as Eli would say, and I wasn't going to pine for that, either.

7

The Kingdom of Ordinary Time

Both of Lizzie's kids had her wispy blond hair and hazel eyes. Maggie, four, and Calvin, one, were buckled into car seats when Lizzie picked me up from the airport. I climbed into the front seat, and Lizzie leaned over to hug me.

"Rach! Hi!" she said.

"Welcome to Denver!" Maggie shouted from the back seat.

"Why thank you," I said, twisting around to face her.

"Excellent greeting, Mags," Lizzie said.

"This is Calvin. He's drinking milk," Maggie said. "I'm eating crackers."

"Here, this is for you," Lizzie said, handing me a snack pack of organic cheese, turkey, and crackers like the one Maggie had. "I brought celery and beet juice, too."

"Awesome!" I said. "Thanks, Mom."

"You called *my* mom *Mom*," Maggie said, and giggled. "That's so silly."

I COULD HAVE FIT EIGHT of my apartments into Lizzie's spacious suburban house. She had things most New Yorkers can only covet from afar: a big backyard with a grill, a king-size bed, a finished basement with a *separate laundry room*.

She set Maggie up at the kitchen table with a Smurfs coloring book and put Calvin in a bouncy seat, then pulled some carrots and hummus out of the fridge and handed me a bottle of white wine to uncork. We headed toward the living room, but before we could sit Maggie shouted, "Mama! I'm going to run over and hug you."

"Come on over, Mags!" Lizzie said, squatting down and extending her arms.

Something about the simultaneous grace and heft of the movement sent me back in time to kid Lizzie the dancer. Lizzie had seemed so comfortable in her body at a time when I was plagued by insecurities about mine: the gap between my two front teeth, my flat chest, my big nose.

Kid Lizzie had long, muscular legs and boundless energy. She emanated a joyful exuberance as a kid that I could see had carried into adulthood. I asked her if she was as at ease in her own body as she had seemed back then.

"Yeah, that's from dancing," she said. "But also because I was raised on a farm in Montana." A llama farm, actually. Lizzie grew up on a *llama farm*.

"I ALSO THINK I inherited that ease from my mom. She was like that, too," she said. When we went to watch Maggie tumble and flip through her weekly gymnastics class later that day, I'd see this quality had been passed down again from mother to daughter.

Lizzie's mom was a music teacher who started Lizzie on the violin at age six; in addition to dance, she'd also played in the orchestra at camp.

"My mom was very type A," she said. "She was a taskmaster, but she also had what's called arteriovenous malformation, and I wonder now how much of her personality was affected by that. It can be anywhere in your body, but it was in my mom's brain; it's where the veins and the vessels are too big and so you get too much blood flow. Hers was like the size of a grapefruit in her brain. It's funny, on the show *Grey's Anatomy* they had two people in there with AVMs. And they both had this crazy sixth sense on the show, and my mom had a crazy sixth sense. Like, once she told me, 'Lizzie, don't wear those shoes today; they're going to get stolen.' And I said, 'Mom, you're crazy,' and I wore them, and sure enough, they got stolen. There were tons of instances like that."

Lizzie's mom died when we were in high school; she was considered a miracle patient to have lived that long.

Despite her mom's teaching music for a living, Lizzie never considered becoming a professional artist of any kind. "I didn't have a plan. That kind of future thinking wasn't instilled in me from my parents. They didn't put pressure on me in that way."

She did get clarity at Interlochen, like every person I interviewed—but for Lizzie, the epiphany was that she wasn't going to pursue dance or any other art professionally.

"I realized I was a minnow next to whales and I was fine with that. Any sense I had of 'I can do this' was shattered, but not in a bad way."

She quit dance and violin after high school and "did the whole pot-smoking sorority sister thing in college." She majored in sociology and history but also sang in a band her senior year. That's how she met her husband, Alan. He approached her one night after their set at a local bar.

"He was a salesman," Lizzie said. "He just walked right over and said he wanted to know me."

They used to play music together, Alan writing songs and mixing tracks that Lizzie sang. But it had been years since they had done that.

"How do you feel about quitting music and dance?" I asked.

"I think I had to," she said. "I vividly remember this high school choir tour I was on in San Francisco. We checked into a hotel and I turned on the TV, and there was Ben Foster. And I remember a sinking feeling, like, '*Fuck*, did I miss the boat? I wish that was me.' I can still see the hotel room even now. And I'm so glad he's had success. It was just this moment of 'holy shit, did I just give up?' I still struggle with it. I recently started playing violin and singing in a band again. I said to my husband, 'Am I good enough?' He was like, 'Oh my god, Lizzie, yes, don't even think about that.'"

I thought back to seeing Ben's movie after filing my taxes and to Daniel talking about Ben's camp performance in *Juvie*. Ben was a touchstone for all of us. We had started out together, and even if we knew better than to compare ourselves to him—given how phenomenal an actor he was as a kid, not to mention the outlier success he had achieved as an adult—it was impossible to fully resist the temptation. I told her about my own path with quitting viola—how I was so shaky with anxiety that first year of college that I lost fifteen pounds.

"You were in a bad place," she said. "It's good you quit."

I'd never summed up my story line so succinctly, and I understood in that moment how part of what I'd needed from this quest to find my old friends was to have someone who knew me back then—who knew how badly I had wanted it and who had experienced her own what-ifs—to release me from my past with such gentle bluntness.

In college, Lizzie started taking Pilates classes, and after she got married, she did an intense yearlong instructor training program in Boulder. Now she taught a few classes a week and stayed home with Maggie and Calvin the rest of the time.

"Why Pilates?" I asked.

"Pilates taught me: you can only do what you can do today," she said. "How do you eat an elephant? One bite at a time. Pilates is not a competition. It's not performance, so why do you do it? Because it feels fucking good. It's good for your soul and your blood and your body and your mind."

"It seems like a natural progression to go from dancing to Pilates," I said.

"What Pilates does is the same as what music does and what dancing does. People who are in tune with their bodies or are good listeners or disciplined are good at Pilates. And the nature of it repels egotistical athletic people, which I love. Which is ironic because Joseph Pilates was actually an egomaniac, racist, sexist asshole. He came over to New York from Germany. He opened up a studio right in Hell's Kitchen, and all of these women and dancers came to him and he hated that. But word had spread that he was sort of a voodoo doctor. If you hurt your knee and had an audition in two weeks, he could fix you."

"Do you think all the training you got in music and dance as a kid was good training for Pilates?"

"I do, but I also think it makes me feel like I'm a totally ordinary grown-up after all that."

"Ordinary how?" I said.

"Like if I just would have tapped into that talent or have known the right person or maybe if I had gone to high school at Interlochen, then I would be someplace else. Feeling that way doesn't rule my life, but it's there."

Despite her complicated feelings, she's still glad she went to camp. It reminded me of how Sarah said she'd send her son if he wanted to go, even after her own disappointments with music.

"Going to Interlochen was good," Lizzie said. "It made me

a stronger person, I think. And I feel like a good dose of reality is important, but it's also important to feel like you have a value and that you're going to make a lasting impression on this earth. In having kids, that's all been put on hold, not in a bad way, in a refreshing way. Seeing the world through their eyes is so amazing. Exposing them to ballet, watching them learn, how quickly they pick things up. I'm totally distracted from that what-if thought by having kids. It's a relief, but I think if I thought about that a lot, I'd be really sad."

Lizzie's open acknowledgment of coexisting with the feeling of what-if seemed radical after I had struggled so long with fighting or reframing that feeling. She made it feel okay to sometimes wonder about what might have been, to feel a little sad that certain parts of your life turned out differently than you'd hoped, while simultaneously being grounded in the fulfilling present of your current life, which for Lizzie centered in large part around raising two kids. I think she was using the term *sad* in the way the philosopher Todd May uses it: "to gesture at something that is less despairing than resignation, less desperate than futility, less backward-looking than regret or remorse, and less intense than anguish."

It's also natural, I think, to struggle with feeling ordinary, like Lizzie did.

"When Alan tells people, 'Oh, Lizzie is such a good singer,' I get so embarrassed," Lizzie said. "I'm like, 'No, I'm NOT.' When he says, 'She plays the violin,' I say, 'I *used* to play the violin.' In my head, I'm saying to myself, *But now I'm ordinary. That's who I am.*"

On Being Ordinary

Ordinary. In other words: average, common, everyday, garden-variety, normal, prosaic, routine, run-of-the-mill, standard, unexceptional, unremarkable, usual. Despite the fact that by definition only a certain percentage of us can be above average at any given task, and the fact that even if we're extraordinary at one thing, we are likely ordinary at *most* other things, *ordinary* is a referendum on how talented or not talented we are, how we have or have not lived up to our potential. A website that plaintively calls itself the Dictionary of Obscure Sorrows even coined a term to describe this feeling: *koinophobia*, the fear that you've lived an ordinary life.

It's difficult to talk about feeling ordinary because our positive-thinking, self-help culture tells us we are all extraordinary, or have the potential to be. We've got entire bookstore shelves filled with offerings like *You Are a Badass: How to Stop Doubting Your Greatness and Start Living an Awesome Life*; *Who Says You Can't? You Do*; *Achieve Anything in Just One Year*; and *Unfu*k Yourself: Get Out of Your Head and Into Your Life*, to teach us how.

The idea of being special taps into something powerful in our psyches (at least mine). It's why as a kid I loved the book *Matilda* by Roald Dahl. Or take the Harry Potter phenomenon. These and other popular stories are about underdog kids who think they are ordinary but realize they are actually special. The idea of moving objects with your brilliant mind or getting a letter from Hogwarts that takes you out of your mundane existence and into a magical, extraordinary one is compelling whether you're thirteen or thirty.

Around the time I met up with Lizzie, I was reading a book about violin prodigies: *Producing Excellence: The Making of Virtuosos*. The author, Izabela Wagner, a sociologist, a musician, and the parent of a talented young violinist, interviewed nearly a hundred prodigies aspiring to become elite international soloists. She observed them at competitions, performances, and lessons. She noted how crucial labels were for these soloists, whether they were referred to as child prodigies or just called very talented or particularly gifted. Wagner argues that both musician and nonmusician parents were susceptible to the "aura" of the talented child, the idea of which has been around since a pint-size Mozart took the stage.

She describes a period of crisis when these kids got older and questioned whether to continue on their path: "For some students with elaborate pedigrees who entered consciousness as 'child prodigies' it is impossible to create a new life project after failure to achieve international soloist status." The virtuosos who instead of becoming soloists ended up as concertmasters or teaching at universities considered themselves failures.

We weren't prodigies, but my friends from Interlochen and I certainly came of age with this "aura" around talent, with parents or teachers who labeled us smart or special or full of potential. This goes for plenty of my nonartist friends, too. And many of us experienced something resembling a period of crisis, whether a fleeting moment or an extended period of feeling lost, when we ventured out into the adult world.

Being special was part of the art monster mythology that had such a tenacious grip on me. To be a successful artist means you have cultivated and monetized your unique talent and vision. It's nothing like the ordinary clock-in, clock-out work lives most people have, we tell ourselves, or like the "ordinary" daily, mostly private achievements of parenting Lizzie experienced. This fear of the ordinary can keep us stuck, though, if we're not careful. When I interviewed Sarah, she told me that two of her close friends wanted to quit music, too, because they were unhappy, but hadn't because nothing else seemed "interesting enough."

SOCIAL MEDIA doesn't help us any when it comes to assessing how interesting (or not) our lives and careers are. Where better to compare our "ordinary" lives to our friends' (and celebrities') curated ones and to ask ourselves on a daily basis whether we measure up? In 2014 Facebook admitted to manipulating the emotional and psychological responses of its users by selectively filtering information on hundreds of thousands of accounts. *Can we make you happy or sad?* was the company's essential question, and since then a slew of articles examining depression, envy, and other emotions linked to social media use have confirmed that the answer is a resounding *yup*. In 2017 Facebook itself even admitted social media might be kinda, you know—depending on how you use it, maybe, yeah—well, almost definitely bad for you. Though they didn't examine whether Facebook could make you feel ordinary per se, we don't really need them to. Everyone I know has enough anecdotal experience to know the answer: also a resounding *yup*.

The idea that we are destined for an extraordinary life plays right into the hero's journey, our favorite Western narrative arc. We are called to adventure; we are tested and tested again and almost give up, but then we ultimately emerge victorious. As the journalist Will Storr, author of *Selfie: How We Became So Self-Obsessed and What It's Doing to Us*, puts it, "the toxic lie our culture gives us is that we can be anyone we want, do anything we want, but that's never been true."

We have been so primed to believe in our own greatness that, if you're anything like Lizzie or me, you're walking around with a sense of loss over not achieving something "bigger." You're both annoyed at your naive self for thinking you were special and simultaneously pissed off that for the most part you turned out to be just like everybody else. I think this is the feeling Lizzie was describing when she wondered what would have happened in her life "if I just would have tapped into that talent or have known the right person or maybe if I had gone to high school at Interlochen—then I would be someplace else."

I found the research of psychologists Hazel Markus and

Paula Nurius helpful for understanding why we can sometimes get lost in this What-If Land. They've written about
how we navigate the world in relationship to our various
selves—our past selves, now selves, and possible selves:
"The individual's collection of self-conceptions and self-
images can include the good selves (the ones we remember
fondly), the bad selves (the ones we would just as soon forget), the hoped-for selves, the feared selves, the not-me
selves, the ought selves." It is our possible selves who are
connected to all those what-ifs. "Possible selves represent an
individual's ideas of what they might become, what they
would like to become, and what they are afraid of becoming."

These various selves influence how we make decisions.
They're also intimately connected with how we think about
our potential—our goals, aspirations, and motives; and
many of "our possible selves are the direct result of previous
social comparisons with others." As Markus and Nurius put
it: "What others are now, I could become." This is why we
measure ourselves against Ben Fosters. It's why Facebook
can make us feel so inadequate. If there was ever an argu-
ment for deleting your social media apps, it might be seeing
the effect on your various selves when you are no longer in-
undated by curated, filtered versions of other peoples'.

At the same time, like giving failure some space, maybe
we should give a little space to acknowledging the loss of
various past or possible selves. Because there is a kind of
loss there. Not a traumatizing one, but the kind of loss
Lizzie was identifying that made her feel a little sad.

I found another psychologist's work useful for understanding that sadness. Dr. Pauline Boss coined the phrase *ambiguous loss* in the 1970s to describe two types of loss: the first is physical absence with psychological presence (anything from a loved one being lost at sea to experiencing a divorce or adoption). The second is physical presence with psychological absence (a loved one with dementia, for example). These are complicated, confusing kinds of losses that resist closure or resolution.

Dr. Boss might be appalled that I'm applying her framework to the mundane adult loss of realizing we are not all going to be Beyoncé. However, we've already established that my methodology for this book is completely subjective, so I'm going to do it anyway.

Boss writes that living with ambiguous loss requires tolerating ambiguity. This is because the "person is still here, but not all here. Part is gone, part remains." I think this describes our past and possible selves. Who we used to be and who we think we can be in the future are both "absent and present at the same time," to use Boss's words. She also writes: "In a can-do society, not being able to find closure is, however, criticized as malingering . . . In cultures where people are socialized to triumph over adversity . . . paradox, compromise, and adaptation are devalued." In other words, ambiguous loss isn't given enough space. I think the same can be said for the ambiguous loss of our various selves. Again, I'm not saying the losses are at all equivalent. I'm simply suggesting that feeling a little sad about saying goodbye to some part of ourselves—our dancer self, our violist self, and so forth—might require a little space, too.

It was clear Lizzie saw her primary "now" self as a mom. It was apparent during the day I spent with her that she was putting a tremendous amount of focused energy into caring for her kids. During my visit, for example, we took the kids to a playground. Maggie noticed a ladybug near the swings and bent down to inspect it.

"Where is she going?" she asked Lizzie.

"Where do you think she's going?" Lizzie asked, sitting down beside her.

"Home," Maggie said.

"Where does she live?" Lizzie asked.

"Over by the slide," Maggie said.

"She's got a long walk, then," Lizzie said.

I sat down, too, and we all watched that ladybug amble along to wherever she was headed. We talked with Maggie about what the ladybug might eat for dinner and how old she was and her favorite color (red, obviously). Together we created a whole imaginary world for that little ladybug.

Creativity researcher Mihaly Csikszentmihalyi's definition of flow is being completely immersed in the task at hand. "Creative individuals are childlike in that their curiosity remains fresh even at 90," writes Csikszentmihalyi. And also: "The first step toward a more creative life is the cultivation of curiosity and interest, that is, the allocation of attention to things for their own sake." Attention. Curiosity. Interest. If this is creativity, that "ordinary" moment on the playground had not only flow, but creative flow. A lot of what I observed of Lizzie's parenting had creative flow, actually. "Do not try to do extraordinary things, but do ordinary things with intensity," artist and writer Emily Carr wrote in her diaries, and I could see that Lizzie was. She was focused, present, and imaginative with her kids. She was creative with them.

We could reject the idea altogether that Lizzie's life as a mom is ordinary. We could say being an engaged, kind, curious parent is an extraordinary feat, the most important kind of achievement, since it involves the fundamental shaping of a human being. Whether you believe this to be true or not, it doesn't fully solve the problem most of us face in various parts of our personal and professional lives of feeling disappointed or ordinary. In those moments, when you're washing your toddler's dishes or changing a diaper for the fifth time that day, it might be more useful to simply acknowledge ordinary is part of the texture of all our lives—and that it can be both beautiful and unsatisfying to experience it, depending on the moment. And to also know that it is okay to feel some sorrow that your creativity has taken a back seat to your children's, to acknowledge that while observing a ladybug with your daughter is a lovely, absorbing endeavor, it is also not the same as spending a quiet afternoon by yourself in a pottery studio or getting to wrangle words into a poem, or performing with your band at a bar, or dancing in front of hundreds of your camp peers.

I got the sense that Lizzie felt like she had run out of time to be extraordinary, like she had all this talent as a kid but stopped cultivating it, and now it's too late. Now it's no longer hers to claim as part of her identity. Now she's just an "ordinary" adult. She doesn't feel comfortable saying she's a musician or a dancer anymore because to do so would feel like grasping at the past, and while she doesn't want to be "ordinary," she feels that being honest with herself means acknowledging that she is.

This is such tricky territory, and, god, I *so* identified with her dilemma. Is the problem with our current cultural conception of ordinary, which has become synonymous with failing to achieve the greatness to which we are all supposed to aspire? Being ordinary means you're one of the invisible masses when you had once hoped to stand out for your talent and achievements. It means your current life does not look like what you think it should look like. It is full of the mundane when it should be full of excitement. Your accomplishments are private, not public. You don't have a million followers; you haven't won a big award; you have no Wikipedia page, no Oscar nominations, no bards composing your legend for the ages.

We can broaden our notions of achievement—not in the Instagrammable, "look at me having it all" sort of way, but in a deeply personal way, an appreciation of the beauty of ordinary moments. This is not magical thinking. It's simply embracing the whole range of experiences, not just the heightened or overtly artistic ones. It's being a curious, observant traveler in your own life. If we broadened our notions of achievement, it would be easy to see Lizzie's life as full of them: a beautiful home, two lovely kids, a kick-ass Pilates body. There were other, less tangible qualities in Lizzie I also admired: the way she was so unselfconsciously grounded in her body, her warmth and openness. The way she was so fully present as a parent.

But broadening our notions of achievement as a way to blunt feelings of disappointment or of ordinariness seems like only part of the solution. Because while I think Lizzie was digging in too hard to this idea of being ordinary—the idea that she had lost her talents because she hadn't kept practicing certain specific ones—her insistence on the idea that she inhabited an ordinary reality was also, I think, a profound and vital way of leveling herself in the world. It was her way of engaging adulthood in a way that felt authentic instead of living in some greatness-in-waiting fantasyland. She wasn't going to fear the ordinary. She was going to claim it. She was determined to be a realist. And realism is *not* the cynical opposite of optimism, no matter what our relentlessly positive culture wants us to believe. I admired that about her, too.

I wished Lizzie could see herself and her life a little more from my perspective, and I also wished I could be a little more like her, fearlessly facing the idea of being ordinary. We are *all* ordinary most of the time in most of what we do, and that's okay. We all have some sparkling qualities that make us stand out as individuals, and it is those sparkling qualities we can cultivate and appreciate while also letting go of the idea that we must shine brightly in every moment in everything we do. All easier said than done, of course. As Heather Havrilesky brilliant put it: "Even once you accept that you're just another regular mortal and not some supernatural force who deserves to live like a fucking

king—a message encoded in the background noise of our daily lives, rich, poor, or somewhere in the insecure in-between—it's still hard not to wish for something more exciting than calm acceptance."

The idea of kid magic fading into ordinary adulthood always makes me think of the epilogue of the final *Harry Potter* book: "Nineteen Years Later." Harry, Ginny, Ron, and Hermione are on platform 9¾ sending off their own kids to Hogwarts. They seem like typical doting parents. Harry and Ron are bantering about parking spots, of all mundane things. In interviews, J. K. Rowling has said that adult Harry became an auror at the Ministry of Magic. I remember reading those final pages of that interview and thinking, *Wait, wait, wait, Harry is a suburban parent with an office job?! What a waste of potential. How ordinary these prodigy kids had become after all their early greatness.*

Only recently have I come to appreciate the ending for what it is. "The scar had not pained Harry for nineteen years," Rowling closes the series. "All was well." Harry had always wanted a stable, loving family, and he got it. Harry wasn't a restless adrenaline junkie perpetually on some hero's individual quest for greatness. His ultimate goal was instead community and connection (things that are easy to lose if we're constantly focused on our individual potential and self-improvement). This is the genius of Rowling's ending. She doesn't give in to heroic fantasies. She offers her readers an ordinary adult reality that is more satisfying and powerful than our fantasies of Harry's future greatness because it is real. Not every moment is life-or-death stakes, and heroes don't have to stay heroes forever. Our identities are not fixed, nor are our callings.

"The Buddhists say that wisdom may be attained by reaching the three marks," writes Jenny Offill in *Dept. of Speculation.* "The first is an understanding of the absence of self. The second is an understanding of the impermanence of all things. The third is an understanding of the unsatisfactory nature of ordinary experience." We can be both fulfilled and a little disappointed. We can be grateful while also longing for something we don't have. Sometimes there is no perfect fix, or maybe the perfect fix is being able to simultaneously hold two contradictory ideas in our heads. As with everything, the trick is balance. I like how Buddhist teacher Pema Chödrön sees that balance: "It happens through some combination of learning to relax where you already are and, at the same time, keeping the possibility open that your capacity, my capacity, the capacity of all beings, is limitless . . . This is the potential of a human being." Now that's a definition of potential I can get behind.

On Uncertainty

Pema Chödrön writes about a lot of the same ideas as Pauline Boss—ambiguity, uncertainty, identity—and what I like about both is that they acknowledge that the very human suffering we feel in relationship to these ideas is totally normal. A friend gave me Chödrön's *Comfortable with Uncertainty* after my divorce, but I didn't read it. After the breakup I needed comedy: Tina Fey's *Bossypants*, Lindy West's take on the movie *Titanic*, that sort of thing. I didn't want to get "comfortable" with uncertainty. I never have, if I'm being honest. Uncertainty is the perfectionist's kryptonite. And I certainly didn't want some New Age Buddhist giving me more emotional homework than I was already giving myself trying to make sense of my wrecked relationship.

And then, super annoyingly, a different friend gave me a copy of Chödrön's *When Things Fall Apart: Heart Advice for Difficult Times*. And I took it as a sign, as I'm prone to do when feeling lost and confused. By then six months had passed and I was no longer spontaneously bursting into tears in cafés and on the subway. I was feeling strong enough to read something other than *Me Talk Pretty One Day* for the fifteenth time.

In *Comfortable with Uncertainty: 108 Teachings on Cultivating Fearlessness and Compassion*, Chödrön writes:

Spiritual awakening is frequently described as a journey to the top of a mountain . . . On the journey of the warrior-bodhisattva, the path goes down, not up, as if the mountain pointed toward the earth instead of the sky. Instead of transcending the suffering of all creatures, we move toward turbulence and doubt however we can. We explore the reality and unpredictability of insecurity and pain, and we try not to push it away.

I felt such a sense of relief when I read those words. Forget *spiritual awakening* and *warrior-bodhisattva*. (Or keep them if you're into that sort of thing.) Here was someone frankly acknowledging suffering and saying the goal was not to transcend it but to lean into it.

In a sea of spiritual self-help, Chödrön is the no-bullshit Buddhist who arrives at your doorstep to tell you that despite your best efforts to avoid pain, you never will. That no matter how much you crave security, you'll never, ever have it. There is no "promise of happy endings." No, you're not ensured success or fame or money or love or children simply because you want them and worked for them. Oh, you're not sure if you want to accept this? Chödrön asks. Cool, fine. But, she writes, you might want to ask yourself this totally-not-at-all-high-stakes question before you decide: "Do I prefer to grow up and relate to life directly, or do I choose to live and die in fear?" Your call, girl. Shrug emoji. Here's what's waiting for you on the other side, though: "This moving away from comfort and security, this stepping into what is unknown, uncharted, and shaky—that's called liberation."

Accepting this uncertainty applies not only to things that happen in our lives but also to our understanding of the various selves researchers Markus and Nurius write about—the identities we construct to make a coherent narrative about our lives. "We have a concept of ourselves that we reconstruct moment by moment and reflexively try to protect. But this concept that we are protecting is questionable,"

Chödrön writes. The goal is to be "less solidly seduced by our Very Important Story Lines."

In other words, you can't avoid suffering, but you can lessen it a little if you don't hold on too tightly to any one idea about who you are: mom, musician, or writer; ordinary or extraordinary. Be flexible with your ideas about yourself. Chödrön is a twice-divorced white woman whose name used to be Deirdre Blomfield-Brown. She grew up in New Jersey and studied English literature at Sarah Lawrence before becoming an ordained nun, so the woman knows a thing or two about the tenuous nature of identity.

When you're a child—regardless of whether you have artistic leanings, whether you are good in math or skiing or sewing, whether you show promise in anything at all—the adults around you are always thinking about your future self. *What are you going to be when you grow up?* We are asked this question over and over. What parents and teachers really want to know is to what will you *devote your working hours?* But for those of us who have been taught to attach our identity to our work, the question is really about our Very Important Story Lines. It is asking us not what we want to do but who we want to be.

At the very least, we should also ask kids: *Where did you get the idea about what you want to be when you grow up? Have you examined it thoroughly, turned it over and over again like a rare gem to identify all its colors and imperfections? Is this idea rigid or malleable? Does it originate inside of you or outside of you, and can you tell the difference?*

I've come to believe that getting too set on any one idea

of our future self is the quickest route to disappointment. We should definitely have goals and aspirations, but we should be flexible as we go after them. Adam Phillips writes about this: "What we learn from experience is that experience keeps stripping us of dearly held beliefs, about ourselves and others. We can't afford to live as though certain things are true about ourselves. Our satisfactions have to be realigned."

We constantly tell kids to be themselves, as if this is a fixed, definite thing, when a much more useful lesson is Pema Chödrön's: We "don't know anything," so let there be room for not knowing.

Chödrön doesn't think you need to be anyone other than who you are right now: "We already have everything we need. There is no need for self-improvement." Sure, you might want some tools for feeling a little bit better about your life. You maybe want to throw down a cushion and meditate, for example, because meditation is one of those tools. But there's no version of you out there living her best life that sad little ordinary you should aspire to be. You don't need a better body, a cleaner house, or an Oscar. You are enough right here, right now, in this beautiful pit of joy and suffering we call life.

The most popular self-help voices today, the ones determined to teach us how to hack happiness and productivity, to dare greatly and fail up, are all working to convince us out of our pain and confusion and loss. You're not ordinary. No, you're greatness-in-waiting. You have endless potential all the time, in all the ways. They want you to think of yourself as a project of perpetual self-improvement; otherwise, how would they make a living telling us how to be better versions of ourselves?

That's why I've come to deeply appreciate when I find voices that go against the grain to say *of course* much of your life will feel ordinary, and of course you will feel frustrated and confused that your life doesn't look the way you envisioned, and that it's not only okay but *the very nature of being human.* It's Adam Phillips describing frustration, Pauline Boss deconstructing ambiguous loss, Rebecca Solnit embracing longing, Todd May talking about sadness, or Pema Chödrön writing: "Who ever got the idea that we could have pleasure without pain? It's promoted rather widely in this world, and we buy it. But pain and pleasure go together; they are inseparable." These voices give us permission to be in whatever moment we're in and to have that be enough.

It is our parents' job to make us feel special. (We could debate just *how* special is good for a kid, but that's another book entirely.) And then we grow up and learn hard lessons about our own insignificance. This is not giving up on your dreams. This isn't accepting mediocrity. This is just declaring a truce with our imperfect circumstances and unmet needs. This is just accepting the ordinary and the fact that in the story line of your own life, you never really know the next plot twist. Growing up is finding the resilience to step into uncertainty and the unknown over and over again. You have to embrace the vulnerability of that. "Start taking off that armor," Chödrön says. "That's all anyone can tell you.

No one can tell you how to do it because you're the only one who knows how you locked yourself in there to start."

Here's what I tell myself these days: There are no guarantees. Anything can happen to anyone. No one is more deserving than anybody else. You don't know what is going to happen. You don't deserve anything more than anyone else or less than anyone else. You are both special and unique and also just another person. And being just another person *is* good enough.

Adam Phillips asks: "What kind of pleasures can sustain a creature that is nothing special?" And I think Pema Chödrön answers him when she writes that the key is being awake to "our pleasure and our pain, our confusion and our wisdom, available in each moment of our weird, unfathomable, ordinary everyday lives."

Lizzie had made an uneasy truce with being "ordinary." She was both fulfilled and also struggled with how her early talent defined her. Sometimes she was sad or disappointed, but it didn't rule her life. She sometimes wondered *what if?* without letting what-ifs dominate her life. She had perspective. I think that's all we can (or should) ask of ourselves.

MY MOM WAS PASSING through Denver in her RV when I visited Lizzie, and I convinced her to come meet up with Lizzie and me for a private Pilates lesson.

"These look like torture devices," my mom said when

she saw the steel frame and straps of the Pilates Reformer machines.

"They won't feel that way, I promise," Lizzie said.

We climbed up on the machines, and Lizzie cranked up the music. She worked us through a series of movements requiring increasing flexibility and strength, gently adjusting us and showing my mom modifications that wouldn't strain her arthritic knee. This was the first time my mom had done any kind of Pilates, so she was understandably nervous.

"Come on, Mama. You, too," Lizzie said whenever my mom hesitated, and I watched my mom brace herself and give it a go. By the end of the lesson my mom was flushed and proud of her efforts.

"I'm going to take some classes back home," she said. "I didn't think I could do all of that—I know I *didn't* do all of it, but the stuff I did do felt really good."

"How do you eat an elephant?" Lizzie asked my mom.

"One bite at a time," she said, smiling.

"Exactly," Lizzie said.

That's all any of us could do. I guess the trick was not getting too frustrated at yourself (or at your elephant) along the way. To stop trying to eat a bunch of elephants all at once. To stop thinking about how ordinary your elephant is compared to someone else's. To maybe stop thinking about your elephant altogether and focus on the eating itself, or to focus on helping your friends and family eat theirs. What could be more beautifully ordinary than that?

8

I Danced Myself Out of the Womb

I finally tracked down Dalia on Facebook. She was using her middle name as her last name, but eventually I spotted her in the friend list of another Interlochen friend. Her page was pretty bare. There were a few photos: Dalia looking pensive on a train in Paris, Dalia giving a thumbs-up while hiking the Ohlone Wilderness Trail in California, Dalia laughing in a blurry Jerusalem night shot. She hadn't posted or captioned anything, just been tagged by other people. Her About section was empty save a single quote: "I danced myself out of the womb."

But when I sent Dalia a message, she was quick to respond: "Holy shit, Rachel! Hi! Yes, I would love to catch up. How have you been these last 20 years?!?"

She was headed to New York for work in a few weeks, so we made a plan to meet. She worked for a research organization, and our mayor had just hired them to evaluate the city's new universal pre-K programs.

AS A KID, I was instantly and intensely drawn to Dalia. She was cool in a totally different way than the sporty, sunny athletes who ruled my middle school back home. She was quietly confident. She chose her words carefully. She was smart, sarcastic, and observant. She brooded, and sometimes her brooding made her inaccessible for brief periods—distracted and solitary. She would sit on her bunk with her journal, scribbling away, emerging once she had worked through whatever was on her mind. She seemed to embrace being sensitive and emotional, whereas I was always worried I was too much of these things. I saw in Dalia the version of who I could be if I didn't spend so much time contorting myself to fit in or worrying about pleasing other people.

Dalia was kicked out of Interlochen two summers in a row. The first time was for smoking in the bathroom with Tamar a few days before the end of camp. The second time, the following summer, was after we had been there only a few days. She had dropped her bags in our cabin and sauntered straight to the bathroom with a tub of hot pink Manic Panic hair dye. The camp's administration was not impressed with the results.

"I remember standing on the little platform in front of the cabin, feeling triumphant, and then I remember a counselor wrangling me to the office, where I got lectured by the head of Intermediates," Dalia said.

We were having dinner at Red Rooster in Harlem. Her hair hadn't been pink for over two decades; it was back to its original blond hue, curling under her ears. She wore huge silver-rimmed glasses that magnified her icy blue eyes.

"Cool glasses," our waitress had said, then asked for our drink orders. Later, when we were putting on our jackets to leave, the hostess also complimented her glasses. I'd realize over the next few months that Dalia was no stranger to fashion compliments. Dalia came back to the city often for work, and every time we hung out, someone always commented on her funky skirt or unique lipstick color or vintage denim jacket. You notice this sort of thing when you (that is to say, me) have zero creativity with clothes and wear the same uniform of black tank top and jeans most days.

"The head of Intermediates told me that I was a negative role model for the other girls," Dalia said. "She said I was on thin ice and that if I so much as had my shirt untucked, they were going to kick me out."

Not long after that, Dalia's counselor found a suicide note she had written. Dalia was immediately whisked off to the infirmary so the nurse could keep an around-the-clock watch over her. Lizzie, Tamar, Sarah, Jenna, and I visited her there, awkwardly milling around, not knowing what to say or do. Eventually our funny, freckled friend Jill, an aspiring actress who grew up to become a high-powered fashion editor, broke the silence by blowing up a latex glove and sticking it on her head like a rooster comb, then loudly squawking around the room. We all cracked up, collapsing in a giggling heap onto Dalia's bed.

Dalia's mom took her home the next day. At least that's

where I always assumed she went. Back to Florida, to palm trees and blue sky, back to her non-Interlochen life. I tried to call her a few times that summer, but her mom always said she wasn't home and she never called me back. The weeks clicked by and then I went home, too, and got caught up in my own non-camp life. I didn't see or speak to Dalia for twenty years.

What I didn't know until we met back up was that Dalia's parents had been unhappily married for years by the time she got kicked out of camp and had recently decided to divorce. But then her father had a stroke and her mother stayed to care for him.

"He was a totally different person for a long time. He was like a child," Dalia said. "I had been acting out at home and then I came to camp and kept acting out."

"I always thought you kind of wanted to get kicked out that last summer," I said. "You seemed so over it."

In the few photos I have of Dalia from that summer, she's sitting to the side of our group, staring off into the distance somewhere or down at the grass. She had gone from brief moments of inaccessibility to being mostly detached.

"I was devastated at getting kicked out," she said. "I loved Interlochen. It was a really rough and confusing time for me."

Dalia didn't intend to commit suicide—that note was a cry for attention—but it scared her mother into sending her to a psychiatric hospital for the rest of the summer, which is why she never called me back. From there, Dalia went to a "therapeutic boarding school" for two years in California.

She wasn't allowed to talk to any of her old friends. When she showed up back in Florida for her senior year of high school, they had no idea where she had been all that time.

"They thought I might have died," she said.

It seemed so obvious in hindsight that the girl I had idolized had struggled just like the rest of us. The way we remember others is always in part about how we construct our own story lines. Then, like now, we're all just trying to figure things out.

AT CAMP, Dalia was an actor and also played violin. She'd been in *Juvie* with Ben Foster, and like Adam and Daniel, she remembered his brilliant performance. Unlike Daniel, though, it didn't make her want to be an actress, and she'd never had an epiphany like Jenna had had while playing the violin.

"I mainly remember being really excited about that play because my character got to wear a tube top," she said, laughing.

By college, she had stopped acting and playing music. She summarized her path from there as "a series of accidents." After high school, she flunked out of the University of Florida and finished her degree at a smaller college closer to home. Then she moved to Texas to get a master's in educational psychology.

"I've never been a planner," she said. "In undergrad, I started off in creative writing, actually. That was my first major. And then I felt a little bit lost and thought, *Oh. I don't know if there are any stories I want to tell, but I really like writing.* So I moved on to journalism, but by that point I had been in school for a while, figuring things out, and I realized that sociology was my quickest path to graduation, so I switched my major again."

She had a charismatic sociology professor and took every class she could with him. Along the way, she got really interested in the problems with standardized tests.

"I thought I wanted to be in research and help undermine standardized testing," she said. "So I went to graduate school, but then after that, I realized I wanted to work at a bookstore again, like I had been doing since high school. I love reading. I love being around books. So that's what I did. But you can't live on that salary."

By then she had moved to San Francisco with a now ex-girlfriend. That's where she met Rebecca, her current partner. A few years into their relationship she quit the bookstore job to travel for six months in France and Israel with Rebecca, another unplanned adventure.

"When I got back to the U.S., finally, I was like, *Okay, I guess I should try to get a job in my field,*" she said.

She was thirty years old, and a job related to her degree seemed like the logical next life step, although she wasn't all that excited to take it. She wanted to feel the passion that had fueled her decision to go to grad school, but it wasn't there anymore. She wanted what she did for a living to be creative and meaningful—she had felt that working at the bookstore getting to read and talk about books all the time. Like many of us, she struggled to balance creativity and practicality: she wanted passion, but she also wanted a decent paycheck. That's how she ended up with the educational research organization that brought her to New York.

The After-Hours Artist

During one of Dalia's visits I mentioned the conversation I had with Lizzie about feeling ordinary. I asked if she ever struggled with that.

"I have this bias where I hold creatives above the rest. But at the same time, if I stop and think about it, I don't really subscribe to that idea. I don't know. I guess I've recently been thinking that I'm not special. Like, nobody is special."

"I've only recently come to terms with the idea that no one cares if I ever write another word," I said.

Dalia smiled. "I never thought anyone cared. It's not up to you whether anyone ever recognizes your art," she said, sounding like Adam. "I don't feel that I need to be an artist in order to be happy, but I think that it's something I want in my life. I have this fantasy of being able to use my free time well enough that I can grow and become confident in my creative pursuits. Like, I took a painting class recently and it was so wonderful."

"What made it wonderful?" I asked.

"I just really, really enjoyed it. There is an intuitive way in which painting makes sense to me. I can intuit: oh, the paint will go this way or that way. It's so rewarding. Regardless of whatever happens it's a way I want to spend my time.

It's like how all through undergrad I took figure drawing classes. I just like the naked body. And I would listen to music and be so focused. Painting and drawing are so engrossing. It's meditative. Typically, I'm so distracted. I'm very, very flighty, and drawing drew me in in this way that felt so calm and . . ." She paused.

"Present?" I said.

"So present, like there was nothing else," she said. "Like I could feel this person's body with the way I was drawing it, if that makes sense. It was just incredible. That's what I'm getting back to now."

"That flow," I said.

"I'm always looking for that flow again, that uninterrupted, consistent movement. In all parts of my life," she said.

Flow is harder these days for me, too, than it used to be when I was a kid. Sometimes it's interrupted by my own negative thoughts and self-doubt. My inner critic is always ready to pipe up with her unsolicited opinions.

And the internet is no friend of flow, in that it is directly hooked up to the very instrument I use to write. Its siren song is always calling, making me believe I must immediately read some new article or tweet. Why yes, I *do* need to know if the benefits of bone broth are overblown. I definitely *cannot live* without seeing that video of "baby dolphin being born swims immediately!" I once spent ten minutes reading an article about how to avoid online distractions before copping to the irony. I have paid services to block my internet. I have put my computer and phone in the bathroom and closed the door, sat down at the kitchen table with pen and paper, and set a timer for three hours. I have signed made-up contracts with myself outlining deadlines and deliverables and given them to bemused friends to hold me accountable. I have tried to live by writer Dani Shapiro's wise warning: *"The Internet is nothing like a cigarette break."* It is not a place where you free up mental space; it's a space where a thousand different things vie for your fragmented attention. But it's still a battle much of the time.

"Why don't you draw anymore?" I asked Dalia.

"Because I lack discipline," she said. "I still make resolutions all the time, like, 'I'll just draw ten minutes every day.' I love drawing. And every once in a while I get into the habit of it and I practice and I have a thousand drawings of my shoes—because those are always in front of me—or my hands. But then I forget and I get home tired from work and I'm like, '*Oh, I need to watch* Parks and Rec.' I just check out."

Checking out, too, takes away from our creativity and flow. Being an adult is *tiring*. We have limited energy, and we don't always know where to direct it. Scheduling time to be creative can feel like one more task on an endless to-do list, not to mention seem antithetical to the organic flow we're craving.

"You had so many creative interests and talents," I said. "Did you ever think about being a professional artist of some kind?"

"Yeah, totally," Dalia said. "I still daydream about it. My mom had a horoscope done for me when I was born, and the person who did it told her I could be whatever I wanted. My mom told me that a *lot*, and it's still stuck in there some-where."

"But you didn't want to pursue acting or violin or draw-ing?" I said.

"I got a lot of positive feedback when I was a kid. With violin, I had a good ear and it came easily to me. A lot of things came easily to me back then. I started ballet when I was two, karate when I was three, violin when I was four. I was always praised for having natural talent. That proba-bly wasn't so great, because if I wasn't immediately good at something I wasn't interested in pursuing it. That's even-tually what happened with the violin and with acting. I remember being very frustrated and having no ability to tolerate frustration and push through it. So that's something as an adult I'm trying to cultivate, and it's really fucking hard. But I'm always looking for creative outlets now. I'm taking a ceramics class. A few months ago I started learning how to cook."

I identified with Dalia's inability to tolerate frustration when I tried out something new. I had recently been trying to learn to cook, too, and I didn't want to be just competent. I wanted to be a skillful improviser, a West Village Nigella Lawson, ready at a moment's notice to host an elegant din-ner party, or, in my less ambitious fantasies, at least to order takeout fewer times a week. Even as I got incrementally better, I found my thoughts constantly returning to the idea that I wasn't a "natural," that I was never going to be one of those people who glances in a cupboard and knows what ingredients can be casually thrown together to whip up a great meal.

I doubt Dalia and I are alone in this space of creative desire mixed with creative frustration, and I think it's why the creativity-in-a-kit movement has recently flourished: things like Blue Apron for cooking, Stitch Fix for fashion, and adult coloring books. Millions of us are yearning for creative outlets and that feeling of flow, and in our high-achiever culture we feel pressure to master whatever we pour our limited resources into, even if it's just for fun.

An Absurdly Brief History of Creativity

Humans' earliest conception of creativity was incredibly narrow in scope. There was only one creator. Yup, you guessed it: God. You don't have to dig any further than Wikipedia to see how ideas of creativity have evolved over time. The ancient Greeks said that in addition to God *fine, okay,* poets could also be considered creators, but NO ONE ELSE. The ancient Romans made another exception for visual artists. But then those killjoy medieval Christians came along and nixed the idea that creativity could be a human activity. Back we went to the belief that the only creator was God. Even poetry was relegated back to being a craft because it was subject to rules and forms. In the Renaissance, the scope of creativity gradually expanded, this time to include various creative arts. Creativity was once again an activity humans could participate in, but only certain kinds of special human beings: artists.

Fast-forward to the twenty-first century: Creativity is no longer just for artists. Now everyone has creative capacity. In the past half century, the science (and pop science) of creativity has exploded. Today cognitive psychologists devote entire careers to understanding creative personalities, creative thinking, and creative achievement. Academic conferences, textbooks, and peer-reviewed journals focus on the topic. Formulas are applied to it.

Current ideas about creativity both help and hinder us, I think. On the one hand, the democratization of creativity means we no longer feel only Rembrandt-level painters should be picking up a brush—which is great. In fact, these days around half of all Americans are pursuing non-work-related artistic activities (painting, singing, music, writing, etc.). But creativity has also somewhere along the way gotten bizarrely intertwined with our cultural obsessions with productivity (unleash the creative entrepreneur inside you!), perfectionism (Blue Apron your way to the perfect meal every time), and public performance (#amcrafting #amwriting #ampainting #amdancing).

Now not only can everyone be creative, but (almost) everyone is. Carrie Battan wrote about this in *The New Yorker*:

"Creative" sits right above "innovation" and "disruption" in the glossary of terms that have been co-opted by corporate America and retooled to signify an increasingly nebulous set of qualities. Consultants are now creative consultants; advertising agencies are now creative agencies. "Creative" was among the top ten most used words in LinkedIn profiles last year, and, these days, "creative" is a noun that can be used for anyone in the workforce who doesn't engage in doctoring, lawyering, writing code, or doing hard labor.

And in the gig economy, Battan notes, we are expected to monetize every creative skill we possess:

If you're learning piano, you must try to record the jingle for that commercial your friend directed. If you develop a curiosity about a niche topic, you must start an online newsletter dedicated to it, work to build your audience, and then try to monetize the newsletter. If you have a nice speaking voice, you must start a podcast. We're encouraged to be "goal-oriented" and rewarded with outsize praise for everything we've accomplished, and so we feel that we need to turn every creative pursuit into a professional one.

That's a lot of pressure to put on creativity. It was that kind of thinking that in part had me stuck when it came to playing viola again. I was always thinking one (or five) steps ahead to the end goal of practicing, how I had to get back to being good again, then back to playing in an orchestra or chamber group, then back to performing.

Everyday Creativity

What I saw Dalia doing was the opposite of this kind of productivity-infused creativity—something more akin to what the psychologist Ruth Richards calls *everyday creativity.* "Throughout our day, whether at home or at work, we humans adapt and innovate, improvise flexibly, at times acting from our 'gut feelings,'" Richards writes. This is everyday creativity, the "originality of everyday life." I think this is what Dalia was striving for when she talked about getting to a place where she used her time well.

To practice this kind of creativity you must cultivate courageous openness to experience and "being freshly and fully present, whether in the garden or the tearoom." Richards also writes that "vocational and avocational creativity" often emerge independently of each other. "One may, for instance, be creative at the office, and come home to relax." To live a creative life you don't have to be creative constantly.

I saw something profound in the way Dalia was practicing everyday creativity that I don't know if she herself recognized. Yes, Dalia had doubts about her life and choices, like all of us. She worried she would get stuck in a job she didn't love. She wished she watched less TV and drew more. She felt like she was lazy and unfocused. But I saw her trying to bypass many of the distractions that can get in the way of uninterrupted time for deep thinking/feeling/

creating. She was mostly unplugged from social media. She wasn't trying to build a platform for her work. She didn't assume she'd ever have or need an audience for her creativity.

The pressure to chronicle our creativity (as part of the pressure to chronicle our lives) has led us to believe that the creative process requires a creative product to share with the world. But Dalia saw being creative as a private pursuit and was focused on the simple but powerful goal of trying to use her time well so that she could experience as many of those moments of creative bliss as possible. If creativity is essentially being present and focused on a task, then the key is simply to protect as much time for it as we can manage from the various distractions in our adult lives.

We all intuitively know how to tap into this everyday creativity. We did it all the time when we were kids and called it play. We just understandably kind of forget how to play when we get older, or we get distracted, or lose confidence or time, or convince ourselves that creativity is worthwhile only if there is a specific creative output attached to it. Dalia had no imaginary finish line in her mind when it came to making something. She was expressing her creativity in lots of little ways all the time, though.

I WONDERED IF DALIA saw herself as a deeply creative person, the way that I saw her. One day I texted to ask her.

"Yes, really and truly," she texted back. "All of my

self-doubt and negative thoughts, when I'm being hard on myself, don't begin to touch this belief. It is something I feel to be in-my-bones-true."

Dalia didn't see creativity as exclusive to the arts. Her creativity came through in painting and pottery classes, yes, but also in making creative choices when picking out her outfits and recommending books to friends. She had found various ways to commune with what she knew about herself to be "in-my-bones-true." And that's as good a definition of fulfillment as any I've ever come across. I'm not talking about anchoring yourself to an identity; I'm talking about figuring out what occupies your full attention when you're doing it. I'm talking about absorption, *flow*. I'm talking about how we spend our time.

"I'm not creative," I've heard certain friends of mine say. Then off they go to train for a marathon (which is at least in part about creatively convincing yourself you can run that far) or they send me a photo of a *Moana* cake they baked for their kid's second birthday, complete with ocean waves made of icing.

Dalia struggled with the idea that artistic people are special. She struggled with feeling frustrated by the limits of her own talents. She struggled with feeling tired from a nine-to-five job and wanting to plunk down on the couch to watch TV. She struggled with life choices and doubts about her career path. She was both satisfied in moments of creative bliss and also frustrated there wasn't more to give to her creative impulses—more time, more focus, more talent, more resources. And she was open to all of it.

DALIA CAME TO NEW YORK a few more times that year. Once we went to a flea market, where she bought what on the rack looked to me like gigantic mom jeans—high-waisted, boxy, unflattering. When she tried them on, we were suddenly in a scene from *Sisterhood of the Traveling Pants* where they fit her perfectly.

Over dinner that night she asked me with a straight face if I had ever thought of getting a chain for my glasses because I kept putting them on and pulling them off to read the menu.

"Um, like an old lady glasses chain?" I said skeptically.

"Yeah!" she said. "Exactly! I think you'd look great."

The days we hung out stretched time like an accordion. We'd meet for brunch at eleven A.M., then realize ten hours later we should probably call it a night. I rekindled friendships to varying degrees with all the people I interviewed for this book, but I got closest to Dalia. She made me rethink entirely what it means to be creative, even though she had moved the furthest of anyone I interviewed from the arts professionally.

It was Dalia who made me understand that creativity wasn't something one could "lose," as I'd always feared. My connection to it wasn't based on my publishing another book or picking up my viola again. It was connected to vulnerability and openness and presence, no matter how I earned a paycheck now or in the future. Dalia also showed me that there is no "real" job versus "creative" job. There is only how you pay your bills and how you enjoy spending your time, and how, if those two things diverge, you bridge that gap in a way that feels at least somewhat satisfying.

Virginia Woolf put it better than I ever could: "[We]—I mean all human beings—are connected with this; that the whole world is a work of art; that we are parts of the work of art. *Hamlet* or a Beethoven quartet is the truth about this vast mass that we call the world. But there is no Shakespeare, there is no Beethoven; certainly and emphatically there is no God; we are the words; we are the music; we are the thing itself."

"HERE'S THE THING about Interlochen," Dalia yelled over the music at some bar we had wandered into during one of her visits. "There was no judgment. You could be passionate and earnest. We all just ran around so enthusiastically. We were all so comfortable. For me, that was its magic."

"You couldn't be earnest back home?" I shouted.

"Definitely not!"

"Do you think we should go back to visit camp?" she said. "Should we get all our friends to have a reunion there?"

"Yes! Let's do it!" I said.

We clinked our glasses to seal the deal.

"I'm not normally this giddy person I am with you," Dalia said. "It accesses some younger part of me, and that feels really good."

Like Dalia, I had lost some kid giddiness as I grappled with personal and professional setbacks: leaving music, getting divorced, struggling as a writer. You know. *Life.* I didn't want to be thirteen again—god no—but I wanted some piece of that girl back. I was giddy with Dalia, too. That was another part of what this quest had been about, I realized—finding a way to be on "nodding terms," to use Joan Didion's phrase, with the kid I used to be, that experimental, vulnerable Interlochen girl. What a feat to pull off if one could do it, becoming a grounded-in-reality-but-still-giddy grown-up.

ONE OF DALIA'S visits was in early fall, still warm enough out to walk around Washington Square Park with our coats unbuttoned, lukewarm coffees in hand. In one corner of the park we stopped to watch a group of enthusiastic college students act out *A Midsummer Night's Dream.* It was the scene where a group of amateur actors perform a melodramatic version of *Pyramus and Thisbe* for the Duke of Athens. The actor playing Robin Starveling stood out from the rest. He was handsome and agile, darting around the other actors and delivering his lines with perfect comedic timing: "All I have to say is to tell you that the lantern is the moon, I the man i' th' moon, this thorn bush my thorn bush, and this dog my dog."

"He's really good," I whispered to Dalia.

"Yeah," Dalia said. "He might just make it."

9

The Ghost Ship That Didn't Carry Us

There was one more person from Interlochen I really
wanted to see. Michelle and I weren't friends back
then, but we were stand partners in the viola section for
much of my time at the camp. We played Bach's Prelude in
C Major and Benjamin Britten's *Simple Symphony* together,
Beethoven's Symphony no. 5 and Fauré's *Pelléas et Mélisan-
dre*. Michelle was incredibly talented. She was my Ben Foster, the person against whom I constantly measured my
own playing. I used to linger outside her practice hut, awe-
struck by her musicality and perfect intonation. Every
summer, competing with Michelle was my daily driving
force.

When I googled her, I learned Michelle was a member of
the Oregon Symphony. Her online bio listed degrees from
top music schools and her solo debut with a professional
orchestra when we were mere seniors in high school. She
had won major competitions and performed all over the
world. She had recorded with indie bands and played at
Carnegie Hall and was part of a hip-looking Portland string
quartet that donated their concert proceeds to charity.

Each new detail I read about her threatened the uneasy truce I had made with my "I coulda been a contender" feeling after more than a year of reconnecting with old friends. But Michelle was different from the others. Except for living in Portland instead of in New York, she enjoyed a musical life that was as close to the fantasy I'd had as a kid as you could get. Despite my best efforts to hold on to my newfound wisdom, I still heard a little voice inside my head whispering: *Hey, girl, you know that could have been you, right?*

I emailed Michelle through the quartet's website. I mentioned that I had family in Portland and was thinking of heading out for a visit (technically true, but also an easier explanation than: *I've been grappling with the idea of childhood potential for the last year, and I'd like to see you in order to hopefully tie things up in a neat "now I'm soooo much wiser" bow*). Michelle wrote back that she was around and happy to chat. I tried to affect a breezy tone in my follow-up email when I mentioned that I was hoping to attend an Oregon Symphony performance. She wrote right back and offered me comped tickets.

THE NIGHT OF THE CONCERT I walked the few blocks from my hotel to the venue. An awesomely gaudy five-foot-tall PORTLAND sign with blaring neon letters illuminated the block. It was a remnant of the hall's bygone days as a vaudeville theater. Inside, ornate chandeliers hung from the gilded lobby ceiling. It was a grand old space, and I couldn't help imagining what it would be like to perform there. For a long time after I quit viola—I'm talking years—I stopped going to classical music concerts because they hooked me right back into that feeling of so badly wanting to be onstage.

The comped ticket put me in the third row in front of the viola section. Members of the orchestra made their way onstage, and Michelle took her seat in the second stand. She looked elegant in a sparkly black top and black trousers, and just as relaxed as she always had when we were kids. She was so close I could hear her individual viola as the orchestra tuned their instruments.

They played Symphonic Dances from *West Side Story*, and then a jazzy saxophone concerto. The third piece was Barber's sad, slow *Adagio for Strings*: a composition I once heard a music historian describe perfectly as a "a melodic gesture that reaches an arch, like a big sigh . . . and then exhales and fades off into nothingness." Up until that moment, I had mostly been focused on watching Michelle play, but during the Barber I was distracted by my visceral muscle memory response to those achingly drawn-out notes. I could feel the radiating discomfort that used to shoot up my right arm. I think the *Adagio* is one of those pieces that will live forever in my body, no matter how many years pass without playing it.

The woman next to me and I were both crying halfway through the piece. So was a man a few seats away. I'm sure we weren't the only ones. The *Adagio* tends to have that effect on people.

MICHELLE WENT TO INTERLOCHEN for nine summers. She started violin at age four and showed remarkable early talent. Neither of her parents were professional musicians, but like Jenna's, both of them were excellent amateur players. Michelle's father was a jazz pianist, and her mother had gone to college on a full viola scholarship.

It was at Interlochen that Michelle started playing viola. The summer she was ten years old the orchestra was short on violists and asked her to switch. And the switch stuck.

"I was already really intense by the time I was eight and went to camp," she told me. We were having breakfast at a café the morning after her concert.

"I grew up in a conservative suburban white community," she said. "I'm black, but I didn't have very many black friends. There is a very strong black community at Interlochen. That was huge for me culturally. I was exposed to different types of music and different types of backgrounds. It was at Interlochen I learned early on there's no one black experience."

Michelle was the youngest kid at camp in 1989. She told me that the camp often sent her to perform for Rotary Clubs and other audiences on the weekends, sometimes two or three hours away. "I had no clue that I was being carted around to show off the camp's diversity and raise money. It was fine, because it was a great opportunity to perform. My counselor would put me in a car with my accompanist. It was mostly those first two years when I was so young and cute."

Michelle loved Interlochen. She remembers bounding out of her car that first summer, barely a glance back at her parents.

"I think about how sheltered I was coming from Ohio," she said. "I was exposed to so much at camp. I don't have sisters. And suddenly there I was with six girls in a cabin! I remember one of my cabin mates was like, 'You don't pluck your eyebrows?' I had no idea what she was talking about. I didn't know gay people before Interlochen. I didn't know what bulimia was. There was so much of the world I had never encountered. Probably the most important thing Interlochen gave me was becoming a more open-minded person."

MICHELLE HAD EXCELLENT EARLY musical training, supportive parents, and boatloads of talent. Her description of how she landed a job with the symphony also made me think she was particularly well suited to the pressure, preparation, and performances involved in her calling.

"Oregon was my sixth or seventh audition," she said. "It wasn't as hard for me as for other people, but it also took a while. People say I got that job fast, but it didn't feel fast for me. My studio was very intense. Now, looking back, I see I had unrealistic expectations."

"Can you describe the audition process?" I said.

"You get onstage and play for members of the orchestra. For the Oregon Symphony, you had to be allowed to play at least a concerto plus three orchestral excerpts before getting voted out. Different orchestras have different requirements, but here five out of the nine people listening have to agree on voting you in. Getting that many musicians to agree on anything is hard. The auditions are completely blind for the Oregon Symphony. The audience is behind a screen. They even put down carpet so you can't hear the person walking in. You don't know if it's a man or a woman. Some people do five auditions before they get a job, and some people do fifty. Some people just don't have the personality to get through that process and they don't know it yet. We take a lot of criticism. If you can't go into an audition and come out and assess your playing over and over again, you're not cut out for this."

In high school, when I started getting nervous before auditions, my viola teacher had me arrive early so I could spend thirty minutes in the bathroom shadowboxing to try to exhaust the nerves that made my bow hand tremble a little when I played. *Jab, hook, cross. Jab, hook, cross.* And then there was college, when those early nerves looked adorably under control by comparison. I never would have made it through the audition process Michelle described. *Never.* I had known that on some subconscious level for a long time, but in that moment it was glaringly obvious.

"Did you always want to be a musician?" I asked her.

"I didn't realize I wanted to be a musician until junior

year of high school. It was then I thought, *Okay, I'll give music a try.* Before that, I was going to be a doctor."

"Do you ever think about doing something else now?" I said.

"I do. I love music, I love playing, but I can see myself doing other things. I'm actually slowly trying to transition into arts management. I've spent ten years playing in the orchestra. I'm ready to try something else. It's hard when people know you as a musician. They can't imagine me doing something else. I've done a lot of administration even here."

I expected someone with as much talent and success as Michelle to be totally attached to her identity as a performer—as if part of what would explain her making it when I didn't was that she had wanted it so much more. We like to think people who succeed have this kind of single-minded focus where they can't imagine doing anything else. Sometimes that's true, but sometimes it's just another story we tell ourselves to explain why someone else got something we wanted.

"Do you remember challenges?" I asked her.

"Oh, of course," she said. "It didn't get intense for me until 1997. That was the first year I lost my chair. I remember that week I had the Concerto Competition coming up. And I won the competition and lost first chair that same week, so I went and practiced like crazy for the rest of the week so I could beat that guy next time."

It didn't take a math genius to realize that if I stopped

going to camp in 1995 and Michelle hadn't lost her chair until 1997, I had never beaten her. How had I forgotten that? I had always thought of us as on relatively equal footing, but we never really were, and my brain had sandpapered over this rough edge. It felt important to acknowledge that—to really sit in the discomfort of that fact.

"Are you okay?" Michelle asked.

Apparently, I was sitting in my discomfort a little too openly. I wanted to ask Michelle a million selfish questions right then. Had I ever been any good? If so, *how* good? Good enough to make it as far as she had? Michelle of all the people I had interviewed would potentially have been able to disabuse me of just how little or much I had inflated my talent over the years, of whether all this time I had confused promise with potential.

But I didn't ask her. It would have felt too embarrassing, too needy, too self-absorbed to assume she had some archived memory of the talent of some kid she barely knew. And besides, it didn't really matter. I knew by now that potential didn't have much to do with what became of your talent. There was so much else at work.

The Road Not Taken

After the concert I had gone out for drinks with Michelle and two of her violinist friends from the orchestra.

"*West Side Story* was all shaky tonight," one of the violinists said, taking a sip of wine. "It never settled."

"Agreed, the whole piece felt weird," the other one said. "And oh god, I came in early in one spot of the concerto, guys. Did you hear it?"

"At least you didn't look like you were falling asleep," Michelle said. "Did you see Ed during the Barber? I swear he was going to nod off." They all laughed.

While the audience had been moved to tears during the *Adagio*, some guy in the viola section had been there and done that so many times that he could barely keep his eyes open. Of course it was like that; even beautiful music could get old once you'd played the same piece enough times, the same as anything could. Like Eli's work at Pitchfork. Like Daniel not getting his screenplays produced. Like Sarah serving at the whim of a petty conductor. Like my hustling as a freelance writer.

Michelle and her friends had been in the orchestra for a decade. It was the first job each of them had landed after college. Orchestras have a tenure system, so often people end up staying with a single one their entire careers.

"We're not the babies anymore," Michelle said. "We're no longer the bright young things. Which is fine, it's the natural evolution of things. But it caught me off guard how quickly that happened."

I had been feeling that evolution, too, as I tracked down my old precocious friends, along with a burgeoning sense of liberation at aging out of potential preciousness.

I loved sitting around with Michelle and her friends after the performance, hearing them dissect the concert and listening to their behind-the-scenes orchestra gossip. Even after all my conversations with old friends, did some part of me still wish I had become a musician? Yup, absolutely. I think a part of me will always long for that, but now I know that feeling is normal and does not require fixing, just acceptance.

Also, I no longer assume that the space between fantasy and reality is as simple as thinking that Michelle got what I wanted. The philosopher Todd May puts it this way:

> I think that, on reflection, most of us would not want to trade with another person, no matter how successful or enticing their lives seem—or even *are* in reality. To see why, though, we'll need to switch our angle of vision. We will have to look at our own experiences rather than at theirs, or perhaps look at our experiences first. What would I be willing to give up to be another? My relationships with everyone—children, spouse, friends—and my whole history. I wouldn't have undergone it. My loss would be that of the whole of my own experience.

May is arguing that you can't pick and choose what to trade for something else in your life without it having a ripple effect on your entire existence. If getting the success someone else has—or the fame or talent or apartment or spouse, or whatever it is that you covet—would require the loss of the "whole of my own experience," well, it becomes kind of unfathomable—at least for me. Nevertheless, writes

Adam Phillips, we are sometimes "haunted by the myth of our potential, of what we might have it in ourselves to be or do." We are haunted by our "unlived lives." If we wander too deeply into those psychological woods, our lives can "become an elegy to needs unmet and desires sacrificed, to possibilities refused, to roads not taken. The myth of our potential can make of our lives a perpetual falling-short, a continual and continuing loss, a sustained and sometimes sustaining rage."

I once read an interview with the actress Sarah Paulson where she summed this up in a way that has stuck probably because I was reared on a steady diet of Julia Roberts rom coms: "I was so busy wanting to be Julia Roberts that it never occurred to me that my career could be something else. And that it could be equally rich, and—the most important thing—it would be mine, whatever it was."

In her famous Dear Sugar advice column, Cheryl Strayed uses language akin to Phillips's when she calls our unlived lives "the ghost ship that didn't carry us." We can never really know how satisfying this parallel life we imagine in our head would be because we haven't actually experienced it, yet we mourn it nonetheless. Strayed writes that this other life is important and beautiful, but also that it is not ours, and thus, she advises, all we can do is "salute it from the shore." This is the same idea, I think, as when Joan Didion writes about being on "nodding terms" with the versions of ourselves we used to be. The people we used to be or might become, the futures we imagine for ourselves—all of that is both real and not real. It both belongs to us and doesn't.

I think what so many of us struggle with are not the impossibilities of our big dreams but the so-close-we-almost-touched-it *possibilities* of them, whether we are comparing ourselves to a famous actor or an old stand partner or whoever else we've decided got some version of what we wanted. We question our choices in those moments. Did we quit too soon? Were we unlucky? Not talented enough? If we can realize it's okay not to have fulfilled our creative potential exactly as we envisioned, we can let go of the fantasy and make room for the much more powerful reality of our lives, including the current creative potential of our adult lives.

Have you read the poem "The Road Not Taken" by Robert Frost? If not, it's short and in the public domain, so here you go:

Two roads diverged in a yellow wood,
And sorry I could not travel both
And be one traveler, long I stood
And looked down one as far as I could
To where it bent in the undergrowth;

Then took the other, as just as fair,
And having perhaps the better claim,
Because it was grassy and wanted wear;
Though as for that the passing there
Had worn them really about the same,

And both that morning equally lay
In leaves no step had trodden black.
Oh, I kept the first for another day!
Yet knowing how way leads on to way,
I doubted if I should ever come back.

I shall be telling this with a sigh
Somewhere ages and ages hence:
Two roads diverged in a wood, and I—
I took the one less traveled by,
And that has made all the difference.

It's been called the most popular American poem in America, as well as the most misinterpreted one. It's often googled with the incorrect title "The Road Less Traveled," which tells you everything you need to know about the nature of its misreading. The narrator takes the "less traveled by" road and says it makes "all the difference." But the narrator *also* says the other road was actually "just as fair" and that "the passing there / had worn them really about the same." In other words, the choice both made a difference and didn't make a difference. I find that ambiguity weirdly comforting—that we must choose a path, but that choosing one doesn't tell us all that much about how our lives might have been different. After all, the narrator doesn't say if it made a positive or negative "difference," simply that it made one.

—————

AFTER BREAKFAST, I got into my rental car and followed Michelle out to a leafy Portland suburb to watch her teach a private lesson. The woman who opened the door looked about our age; she had cheese and crackers waiting for us, as if it wasn't already generous enough to let a stranger sit on your couch with your purring cat and observe you work your way through Hindemith's Viola Concerto.

Coincidentally, Michelle's student had also gone to Interlochen as a kid, although our summers there didn't overlap. She quit viola after college. She got a job in marketing, got married, and bought this lovely Portland home.

"What made you decide to start playing again?" I asked her.

"I always loved playing. I wanted to see what it would be like to try again," she said.

"To try what, exactly?" I pressed.

"Just to practice. I'm learning how to practice again," she said.

There's a beautiful memoir by Glenn Kurtz, aptly titled *Practicing,* in which he describes his journey back to the guitar years after he decides to stop being a professional musician. He articulates so perfectly how I felt about quitting viola, the heartbreak and then the intense frustration of trying to play again years later. Slowly he figures out how to practice without his ego getting in the way. By the end of the book, his love of guitar has been rekindled. The trick, he writes, is letting go of the past and realizing you "must make the music of today."

I read *Practicing* when I was just starting work on this book, and I thought that my journey would end up resembling Kurtz's and Michelle's student. I'd find my way back to playing viola, but this time with a new, more enlightened perspective.

I did finally go to one of those community orchestra rehearsals. But it was a torturous few hours. I was not only rusty but also way too in my head worrying about how I sounded. I never went back, and I've let myself off the hook for that. Sometimes a broken thing stays broken, and the lesson I learned instead was that I needed to let go of playing viola once and for all. I needed to say goodbye to my viola-playing self and appreciate what she had given me for many years: creative expression, community, joy, discipline, and an enduring love of music. She had also been instrumental in preparing me to be a writer. Without her, who knows what unlived life I might be leading, and I had learned to value the one I had precisely because it was mine. I had built it, brick by hard-earned wisdom brick.

THE PAST FEW MONTHS I *have* been learning to practice again, though. I started taking group guitar lessons, and it has been *so* much fun. Once a week I show up to a Midtown studio for my lesson and muddle my way through Coldplay and Johnny Cash and the Beatles.

John, the bald, bearded instructor, approached me one day as I was packing up. I'd been taking lessons for a few months by then.

"You know, you're pretty good," he said. "Have you thought about performing?"

Had I thought about performing? Of *course* I had thought about performing. I had many a night drifted off to sleep fantasizing about being onstage with my band in front of thousands of fans who were cheering and singing along.

I don't think I'll ever stop fantasizing about my unlived life as a musician in some form or another, whether I'm belting out show tunes at a piano bar or seeing live music or taking guitar lessons. But the fantasies don't hook me into a darker what-if place with guitar. My ego isn't deeply invested in that instrument like it was with the viola. I mostly just want to practice, and that, as Lizzie would say, feels fucking *good*.

"Nope," I said to John, sticking my pick between the top three strings of the same guitar I had played as a kid a million years ago. I shut the case. "But I'll see you next week."

CODA

I didn't go back to Interlochen as an adult as Dalia and I had talked about. I realized I didn't want to experience that inevitable moment of surreal shock from how small the cabins were or how young the kids all seemed or whatever else would alter my memories. I had already cracked open enough of my childhood self. I had dismantled enough of the magic of that time. I didn't want to blow off every speck of fairy dust.

I did, however, keep in touch with most of my old friends. Jenna had a second kid and is still teaching. Tamar moved back to her hometown. I don't know if she's acting, but she looks really happy on Instagram. Adam got married and sold a screenplay. Sarah had a second kid and decided to take a break from teaching. Eli took a staff job and then quit to freelance again. He recently married his girlfriend of eleven years. Daniel has been promoted at his company. Lizzie still teaches Pilates and now CycleBar, too. Dalia quit her job at the research organization to work at a co-op bakery. Michelle took a yearlong sabbatical from the orchestra to take a fellowship in arts administration. And me—well, I wrote this book.

I still worry. I still struggle with how to live a fulfilling artistic life, a question that has taken on wildly new dimensions since having a kid. (I really buried the lede with the kid thing, didn't I?) Some days I feel content and satisfied. Other days not so much. But the moments I feel disappointed or frustrated don't overwhelm me the same way they did before I reckoned with my Cadillac problem of potential. I have a little distance and much more acceptance of these feelings. I am more at ease with the contradiction that my life is wonderful and also that it is imperfect. That I am both special and ordinary. I know now that gratitude and longing can co-exist. That I can be both a little lost and also on the right path.

These are my takeaways, of course. We each have to find our own, and there are no shortcuts no matter how well traveled the road you choose. Although, if you've got any old friends who knew you back when you knew you, too, I'd say that's as good a place to start as any.

ACKNOWLEDGMENTS

Thank you to Marisa Vigilante and Colleen Lawrie for being wonderful friends and thoughtful early readers/editors. You were instrumental in helping me shape the idea for this book, and your belief in it means everything to me. Anna Sproul-Latimer is the best, bluntest, smartest agent in the world. Thanks for your real talk and limitless moral support. I hope you don't regret giving me your cell phone number. Meg Leder at Penguin Books has been a brilliant and patient editor. This book is so much better for having her in its life. Thanks, Meg, and Shannon Kelly, for your invaluable insights and guidance. And thanks to the rest of the Penguin team: Kathryn Court, Patrick Nolan, Kate Stark, Lydia Hirt, Allison Carney, Maya Baran, Ciara Johnson, Matt Giarratano, Nicole Celli, Nancy Inglis, and Lynn Buckley.

Thank you to friends, family, and colleagues who supported me in various ways as I wrote this book: Carly Dawson, Robin Yudkovitz, Michelle Schackman, Danielle Romeo, Jaci Colby, Stephanie Psaki, Jane Segal, Erica Gaetano, Lavinia Spalding, Meredith Friedman, Amy Bruno, Jessica Pitt, Marc and Jessica Friedman, Rae-Ellen Kavey, Christina Tse, Mechelle Chestnut, Sonia Ramirez, Barbara Sanchez, and Gresha Ellington. It's going to be horrifying six months from now when I realize I've inadvertently left someone off this list . . .

I wrote much of *And Then We Grew Up* in the Frederick Lewis Allen Memorial Room in the New York Public Library. If you are reading this, please stop and immediately go donate money, books, time, hand-churned butter, or whatever else your local library needs. These are invaluable spaces for readers, writers, and communities.

Thank you to my parents, Lester and Carolyn, who instilled in me a deep love for the arts and drove me to countless music lessons as a kid. I must also thank my son, Eben, who is almost three years old as I write these acknowledgments. E, you have taught me so much about growing up and about everyday creativity. My wish for you: may you get satisfying amounts both of what you want and what you need in life, and most crucially, may you cultivate the wisdom to know the difference.

Finally, my deepest appreciation to my Interlochen friends. Getting to know you again as adults has been such a joy. I cannot thank you enough for welcoming me into your homes and lives. There would be no book without you.

NOTES

Chapter 1: Potential

19 Maslow's hierarchy of needs: "Maslow's Hierarchy of Needs." Wikipedia, January 3, 2019; https://en.wikipedia.org/wiki/Maslow's_hierarchy_of_needs.

19 "to become more and more what one is": Abraham Maslow, *Motivation and Personality* (New York: Harper & Brothers, 1954).

19 "Cadillac problems": Rachel Cooke, "Interview with Rebecca Solnit: 'The Essay Is Powerful Again. We're in a Golden Age.'" *The Guardian*, August 27, 2017.

Chapter 2: I Was Going to Be an Art Monster Instead

28 Jenny Offill's brilliant novel *Dept. of Speculation*: Jenny Offill, *Dept. of Speculation* (New York: Knopf, 2014), 8.

28 "I'm actively working": Paul Zollo, *Songwriters on Songwriting* (New York: Da Capo Press, 2003), 349.

29 "My fear of life is necessary to me": Arthur Lubow, "Edvard Munch: Beyond the Scream." *Smithsonian Magazine*, March 2006.

29 worried about how mental illness would hinder: Kate Stone Lombardi, "Exploring Artistic Creativity and Its Link to Madness." *The New York Times*. April 27, 1997; https://www.nytimes.com/1997/04/27/nyregion/exploring-artistic-creativity-and-its-link-to-madness.html.

29 The idea of the tortured artist: Allan Beveridge, "A Disquieting Feeling of Strangeness?: The Art of the Mentally Ill." *Journal of the Royal Society of Medicine* 94, no. 11 (2001): 595–99.

29 "unbalanced views should be kept, as far away from religion and politics as possible": Adam Phillips, *On Balance* (New York: Farrar, Straus and Giroux, 2010), xii.

30 **"There is a great deal ... work"**: Susan Sontag, edited by David Rieff, *As Consciousness Is Harnessed to Flesh: Diaries, 1964–1980* (London: Penguin, 2012), 487.

31 **"very much of this world"**: *Nanette*, released on Netflix in 2018.

33 **"first reader ... the implacable guardian of his legacy"**: Judith Thurman, "Silent Partner: What Do Nabokov's Letters Conceal?" *The New Yorker.* November 8, 2015; https://www.newyorker.com /magazine/2015/11/16/silent-partner-books-judith-thurman.

34 **"need support from significant others"**: Izabela Lebuda and Mihaly Csikszentmihalyi, "All You Need Is Love: The Importance of Partner and Family Relations to Highly Creative Individuals' Well-Being and Success." *Journal of Creative Behavior* (2018). DOI: 10.1002/jocb.348.

36 **"In the long run we are all dead"**: Diana Athill, Margaret Atwood, Julian Barnes, Anne Enright, Howard Jacobson, Will Self, and Lionel Shriver, "Falling Short: Seven Writers Reflect on Failure." *The Guardian,* June 22, 2013; https://www.theguardian.com /books/2013/jun/22/falling-short-writers-reflect-failure.

Chapter 3: On "Making It"

48 **the median pay for actors is $17.49 per hour:** "Actors: Summary." U.S. Bureau of Labor Statistics. April 13, 2018; https:// www.bls.gov/ooh/entertainment-and-sports/actors.htm.

48 **for full-time writers it's $20,000 a year:** Concepción de León, "Does It Pay to Be a Writer?" *The New York Times.* January 5, 2019; https://www.nytimes.com/2019/01/05/books/authors-pay -writer.html.

48 **out of two million arts graduates:** Susan Jahoda, Blair Murphy, Vicky Virgin, and Caroline Woolard, *Artists Report Back: A National Study on the Lives of Arts Graduates and Working Artists.* BFAMFAPhD .2014; http://bfamfaphd.com/wp-content/uploads/2016/05/BFAMFA PhD_ArtistsReportBack2014-10.pdf.

51 **"This is social media's basic Faustian pact"**: Ruth Whippman, *America the Anxious: How Our Pursuit of Happiness Is Creating a Nation of Nervous Wrecks* (New York: St. Martin's Press, 2016), 167.

51 **"Everybody loves the underdog"**: "Egos Like Hairdos" by Ani DiFranco, *Puddle Dive,* Righteous Babe Records, 1993.

53 **"Common sense suggests"**: Adam Grant, *Originals: How Non-Conformists Move the World* (New York: Penguin Books, 2017), 19.

53 *Big Magic: Creative Living Beyond Fear:* Elizabeth Gilbert, *Big Magic: Creative Living Beyond Fear* (New York: Riverhead Books, 2015).

53 **such as the composer Philip Glass:** Clay Wirestone, "11 Celebrated Artists Who Didn't Quit Their Day Jobs," *Mental Floss,* August 11, 2018; http://mentalfloss.com/article/52293/11-celebrated-artists-who-didnt-quit-their-day-jobs.

55 **"committed above all"**: Adam Phillips, *Missing Out: In Praise of the Unlived Life* (New York: Picador/Farrar, Straus and Giroux, 2012), xiv.

60 **"view their careers as a checkerboard"**: Sarah Thornton, *33 Artists in 3 Acts* (London: Granta, 2015).

62 **"I refused . . . special prerogatives and special excuses"**: Anne Truitt, *Daybook* (London: Simon & Schuster, 2013), 17.

62 **"more alive than the others"**: Agnes de Mille, *Martha: The Life and Work of Martha Graham* (New York: Random House, 1991). Thanks to Brainpickings.org for leading me to this work.

65 **"I can't write the book I want to write"**: Ann Patchett, *This Is the Story of a Happy Marriage* (New York: Harper, 2013), 30.

65 **"the practice *is* the art"**: Dani Shapiro, *Still Writing: The Pleasures and Perils of a Creative Life* (New York: Atlantic Monthly Press, 2013), 51.

66 **"The idea that excellence at performing a complex task"**: Malcolm Gladwell, *Outliers: The Story of Success* (New York: Back Bay Books/Little, Brown, 2013), 39–40.

67 **Ericsson and his colleagues proposed:** K. Anders Ericsson, Ralf T. Krampe, and Clemens Tesch-Römer, "The Role of Deliberate Practice in the Acquisition of Expert Performance." *Psychological Review* 100, no. 3 (1993): 363–406; doi:10.1037/0033-295x.100.3.363.

67 **He has said Gladwell misinterprets:** Anders Ericsson and Robert Pool, "Malcolm Gladwell Got Us Wrong: Our Research Was Key to the 10,000-Hour Rule, but Here's What Got Oversimplified." *Salon,* April 10, 2016; https://www.salon.com/2016/04/10/malcolm_gladwell_got_us_wrong_our_research_was_key_to_the_10000_hour_rule_but_heres_what_got_oversimplified.

68 **"Great question"**: Anders Ericsson, telephone interview with the author, May 1, 2017.

68 **"I think Anders Ericsson"**: Ellen Winner, telephone interview with the author, May 16, 2017.

69 **"But people and human performance [are] complex":** Brooke Macnamara, telephone interview with the author, April 25, 2017.

70 **"and not necessarily even the largest piece":** David Z. Hambrick, Brooke N. Macnamara, Guillermo Campitelli, Fredrik Ullén, and Miriam A. Mosing, "Chapter One—Beyond Born Versus Made: A New Look at Expertise." *Psychology of Learning and Motivation* 64 (2016): 1–55; doi.org/10.1016/bs.plm.2015.09.001.

70 **when we spoke on the phone:** Zach Hambrick, telephone interview with the author, April 25, 2017.

73 ***Grit: The Power of Passion*:** Angela Duckworth, *Grit: The Power of Passion and Perseverance* (New York: Scribner, 2018), 8.

74 **David Denby wrote in *The New Yorker*:** David Denby, "The Limits of 'Grit.'" *The New Yorker,* June 21, 2016; https://www.newyorker.com/culture/culture-desk/the-limits-of-grit.

75 **In the UK, artists are mostly from the middle class:** Hannah Ellis-Petersen, "Middle Class People Dominate Arts, Survey Finds." *The Guardian,* November 23, 2015; https://www.theguardian.com/artanddesign/2015/nov/23/middle-class-people-dominate-arts-survey-finds.

75 **A mere 16 percent are from working-class backgrounds:** Gloria De Piero and Tracy Brabin, "Privilege Is Playing Too Great a Role in the Arts." *The Guardian,* February 11, 2017; https://www.theguardian.com/commentisfree/2017/feb/11/acting-class-privilege-stage.

75 **In the United States, Createquity did a recent analysis:** Shawn Lent, Louise Geraghty, Michael Feldman, Talia Gibas, and Ian David Moss, "Who Can Afford to Be a Starving Artist?" Createquity, June 14, 2016; http://createquity.com/2016/06/who-can-afford-to-be-a-starving-artist.

75 **The average family income of someone who graduates with a BFA:** Shawn Lent, Louise Geraghty, Michael Feldman, and Talia Gibas, "The BFA's Dance with Inequality." Createquity, May 25, 2016; http://createquity.com/2016/05/the-bfas-dance-with-inequality.

75 **"less likely to have access to arts education":** Anne O'Brien, "How to Close the Achievement Gap: Arts Education." Edutopia, September 11, 2013; https://www.edutopia.org/blog/art-education-closing-achievement-gap-anne-obrien.

76 **"three times more likely"**: "Research That Suggests Art Can Close the Achievement Gap Between Low and High Socioeconomic Groups." Americans for the Arts Action Fund, April 5, 2012; http://www.artsactionfund.org/news/entry/research-that-shows-art-can-close-the-achievement-gap-between-low-and-high-.

76 **"'Do what you love and the money will follow'"**: *Scratch: Writers, Money, and the Art of Making a Living,* ed. Manjula Martin (New York: Simon & Schuster, 2017), xiii, 61, 102.

77 **You don't have to look:** Jennifer Medina, Katie Benner, and Kate Taylor, "Actresses, Business Leaders and Other Wealthy Parents Charged in U.S. College Entry Fraud." *The New York Times,* March 12, 2019; https://www.nytimes.com/2019/03/12/us/college-admissions-cheating-scandal.html?module=inline.

77 **"believe firmly enough in the inevitability of your success":** Barbara Ehrenreich, *Bright-Sided: How the Relentless Promotion of Positive Thinking Has Undermined America* (New York: Metropolitan Books, 2009), 8.

77 **"believing that success":** Judith Halberstam, *The Queer Art of Failure* (Durham, NC: Duke University Press, 2011), 3.

78 **Take a recent study on the relationship between wealth and luck:** Emerging Technology from the arXiv, "If You're So Smart, Why Aren't You Rich? Turns Out It's Just Chance." *MIT Technology Review,* March 1, 2018; https://www.technologyreview.com/s/610395/if-youre-so-smart-why-arent-you-rich-turns-out-its-just-chance.

78 **"It's a really important word":** Stuart Firestein, "The Resulting Fallacy Is Ruining Your Decisions." *Nautilus,* issue 055, Trust, December 7, 2017; http://nautil.us/issue/55/trust/the-resulting-fallacy-is-ruining-your-decisions.

81 **"awful, beautiful, knowing mask":** "Collection." https://www.artgallery.nsw.gov.au/collection/works/154.2011.14.

83 **"I am not going . . . a kind of fairy tale resolution":** J. K. Rowling, "Text of J. K. Rowling's Speech." *Harvard Gazette,* June 5, 2008; https://news.harvard.edu/gazette/story/2008/06/text-of-j-k-rowling-speech.

83 **"to work really hard at what we love":** Heather Havrilesky, "Ask Polly: Should I Just Give Up on My Writing?" *The Cut,* September 16, 2015; https://www.thecut.com/2015/09/ask-polly-should-i-just-give-up-on-my-writing.html.

Chapter 4: Never Quit! (But Maybe Quit)

89 **Jazz players popularized the term:** Robert S. Gold, *A Jazz Lexicon* (New York: Knopf, 1964).

89 **One of the meanings of *gig* as a verb:** "Gig." Merriam-Webster, https://www.merriam-webster.com/dictionary/gig.

89 **In 2011, my hometown orchestra filed for bankruptcy:** Michelle Breidenbach, "Syracuse Symphony Orchestra Files for Bankruptcy." Syracuse.com, May 10, 2011; https://www.syracuse.com /news/index.ssf/2011/05/syracuse_symphony_orchestra_fi.html.

89 **There have been strikes:** Maggie Severns, "Are City Orchestras a Dying Breed?" *Mother Jones,* February 4, 2013; https://www .motherjones.com/media/2013/02/are-orchestras-dying -minnesota-lockout.

89 **"It's Official: Many Orchestras Are Now Charities":** Michael Cooper, "It's Official: Many Orchestras Are Now Charities." *The New York Times,* November 15, 2016; https://www.nytimes.com/2016/11 /16/arts/music/its-official-many-orchestras-are-now-charities.html.

90 **"There are 117 major symphony orchestras":** Drjonesmusic, "Music and Economics." Dr. Jones' Music Classes, November 5, 2018; https://drjonesmusic.me/2018/11/05/music-and-economics.

91 **a study of over two thousand professional musicians:** Sally Anne Gross and George Musgrave, *Can Music Make You Sick? Music and Depression: A Study into the Incidence of Musicians' Mental Health.* Report, University of Westminster/MusicTank, November 2016; https:// westminster research.westminster.ac.uk/download/fd3b380d63e4e4a 1219017768f5a56a2004e0916b59065565bac67b9d9562a22/3955058 /Gross%20%26%20Musgrave%20%282016%29%20Can%20Music %20Make%20You%20Sick%20Pt1.pdf.

91 **"pathetically unequipped children":** Joan Didion, *Slouching Towards Bethlehem: Essays* (New York: FSG Classics, 2017), 122.

91 **"For Americans under the age of 40":** David Leonhardt, "The Fleecing of Millennials." *The New York Times,* January 27, 2019; https:// www.nytimes.com/2019/01/27/opinion/buttigieg-2020-millennials .html.

91–92 **We have more debt than our parents . . . "as much money as their parents did":** David Leonhardt, "The American Dream, Quantified at Last." *The New York Times,* December 8, 2016; https://

www.nytimes.com/2016/12/08/opinion/the-american-dream
-quantified-at-last.html.

92 **The journalist Scott Timberg:** Scott Timberg, "The Creative
Class Is a Lie." *Salon,* October 1, 2011; https://www.salon.com/2011
/10/01/creative_class_is_a_lie.

93 **"Much of the economic infrastructure":** Scott Timberg, email
interview with the author, December 23, 2015.

94 **"We have to be attentive":** Phillips, *Missing Out,* 141.

96 **"We tell ourselves stories in order to live":** Joan Didion, *The
White Album: Essays* (New York: FSG Classics, 2009), 11.

96 **"you never fail until you stop trying":** Kevin Daum, "23
Genius Quotes from Albert Einstein That Will Make You Sound
Smarter." Inc.com, March 14, 2016; https://www.inc.com/kevin
-daum/26-genius-quotes-from-albert-einstein-that-will-make-you
-sound-smarter.html.

97 **"We all came from high schools where we were all the
exception":** Jessica Bennett, "On Campus, Failure Is on the
Syllabus." *The New York Times,* June 24, 2017; https://www.nytimes
.com/2017/06/24/fashion/fear-of-failure.html.

98 **In a survey of 275 counseling centers:** Robert P. Gallagher,
National Survey of College Counseling Centers 2014. University of
Pittsburgh. International Association of Counseling Services; http://
d-scholarship.pitt.edu/28178.

98 **And anxiety is the most common concern:** Peter LeViness,
Carolyn Bershad, and Kim Gorman. *The Association for University and
College Counseling Center Directors Annual Survey, July 1, 2016, through
June 30, 2017;* https://www.aucccd.org/assets/2017%20aucccd
%20survey-public-apr17.pdf.

98 **"dispatches from young people":** Heather Havrilesky, *What If
This Were Enough? Essays* (New York: Doubleday, 2018), 115.

99 **"We reckon our incomes once a year":** Scott A. Sandage, *Born
Losers: A History of Failure in America* (Cambridge, MA: Harvard
University Press, 2006), 265.

101 **"whether it causes a stir or not":** Maria Popova, "To Paint Is to
Love Again: Henry Miller on Art, How Hobbies Enrich Us, and
Why Good Friends Are Essential for Creative Work." Brain Pickings,
January 21, 2015; https://www.brainpickings.org/2015/01/21
/to-paint-is-to-love-again-henry-miller.

102 **"slightly less lacerating vulnerability"**: Todd May, *A Fragile Life: Accepting Our Vulnerability* (Chicago: University of Chicago Press, 2017), viii.

103 **Oprah once asked Eckhart Tolle**: "Eckhart Tolle: Being in the Now." *Oprah's SuperSoul Conversations*, July 23, 2018; https://podtail .com/en/podcast/oprah-s-supersoul-conversations/eckhart-tolle -being-in-the-now.

103 **"relentless optimism"**: Ehrenreich, *Bright-Sided*, 202.

103 **"The real problems"**: Ruth Whippman, *America the Anxious: How Our Pursuit of Happiness Is Creating a Nation of Nervous Wrecks* (New York: St. Martin's Press, 2016), 196.

104 **"'Fail better' means"**: Pema Chödrön, *Fail, Fail Again, Fail Better* (Boulder, CO: Sounds True, 2015), 115, 71, 61.

106 **"At least 12 are out of professional music"**: Daniel J. Wakin, "The Juilliard Effect: Ten Years Later." *The New York Times,* December 12, 2004; https://www.nytimes.com/2004/12/12/arts /music/the-juilliard-effect-ten-years-later.html.

110 **"They can quit too early"**: "The Upside of Quitting." *Freakonomics* (transcript), September 30, 2011; http://freakonomics.com/2011/09 /30/the-upside-of-quitting-full-transcript.

Chapter 5: Freedom's Just Another Word

123 **"People are often told to find their passion"**: Paul A. O'Keefe, Carol S. Dweck, and Gregory M. Walton, "Implicit Theories of Interest: Finding Your Passion or Developing It?" *Psychological Science* 29, no. 10 (2018): 1653–664. doi:10.1177/0956797618780643.

123 **Though I feel compelled to note**: Carl Hendrick, "The Growth Mindset Problem." Aeon.co, March 11, 2019; https://aeon.co/essays /schools-love-the-idea-of-a-growth-mindset-but-does-it-work.

123–124 **openness to experience**: Ruth Richards, *Everyday Creativity and the Healthy Mind: Dynamic New Paths for Self and Society* (Basingstoke, Hampshire: Palgrave Macmillan, 2018).

130 **"Writing is hard . . ."**: "Dear Sugar, The Rumpus Advice Column #48: Write Like a Motherfucker." The Rumpus, August 19, 2010; https://therumpus.net/2010/08/dear-sugar-the-rumpus-advice -column-48-write-like-a-motherfucker.

Chapter 6: Never Compromise! (But Definitely Compromise)

139 **an unproduced screenplay has about a 0.3 percent chance:** Scott Meslow, "How Hollywood Chooses Scripts: The Insider List That Led to 'Abduction.'" *The Atlantic*, September 23, 2011; https://www.theatlantic.com/entertainment/archive/2011/09/how-hollywood-chooses-scripts-the-insider-list-that-led-to-abduction/245541.

151 **"I had erred not only in my prediction":** Jesse Browner, *How Did I Get Here?: Making Peace with the Road Not Taken* (New York: HarperWave, 2015), 72.

152 **"The 'second career' is an illusion!":** Brassaï, *Conversations with Picasso* (Chicago: University of Chicago Press, 2002), 179.

152 **"the best work in literature is":** Nadia Khomami, "Literary Success? Don't Give up the Day Job, Advised Oscar Wilde." *The Telegraph*, March 19, 2013; https://www.telegraph.co.uk/culture/books/9939664/Literary-success-Dont-give-up-the-day-job-advised-Oscar-Wilde.html.

152 **"are faced with a stark":** Browner, *How Did I Get Here?*, 204.

153 **unasked for out of my heart and mind and mouth and gut:** Charles Bukowski, "So You Want to Be a Writer?" Poets.org, April 10, 2014; https://www.poets.org/poetsorg/poem/so-you-want-he-writer.

153 **"If this was quantifiable we would say":** Phillips, *Missing Out*, 30.

154 **"for something of this longing will, like the blue of distance":** Rebecca Solnit, *A Field Guide to Getting Lost* (New York: Penguin Books, 2006), 30–31.

Chapter 7: The Kingdom of Ordinary Time

157 **The Kingdom of Ordinary Time:** The title of this chapter is a reference to Marie Howe's book *The Kingdom of Ordinary Time: Poems* (New York: W. W. Norton, 2009).

163 **"to gesture at something that is less despairing":** May, *A Fragile Life*, 192.

165 ***Producing Excellence: The Making of Virtuosos:*** Izabela Wagner, *Producing Excellence: The Making of Virtuosos* (New Brunswick, NJ: Rutgers University Press, 2015).

166 **In 2014 Facebook . . . selectively filtering information:** Vindu
Goel, "Facebook Tinkers with Users' Emotions in News Feed
Experiment, Stirring Outcry." *The New York Times,* June 29, 2014;
https://www.nytimes.com/2014/06/30/technology/facebook-tinkers
-with-users-emotions-in-news-feed-experiment-stirring-outcry
.html.

167 **In 2017 Facebook itself even posted a blog:** Sam Levin,
"Facebook Admits It Poses Mental Health Risk—but Says Using Site
More Can Help." *The Guardian,* December 15, 2017; https://www
.theguardian.com/technology/2017/dec/15/facebook-mental-health
-psychology-social-media.

167 **"the toxic lie our culture gives us":** Sean Illing, "How the West
Became a Self-Obsessed Culture." Vox.com, July 19, 2018; https://
www.vox.com/science-and-health/2018/7/19/17518086/selfie-will
-storr-book-psychology-west.

167–68 **the research of psychologists Hazel Markus and Paula
Nurius:** Hazel Markus and Paula Nurius, "Possible Selves." *American
Psychologist* 41, no. 9 (September 1986): 954–69; doi:10.1037/0003
-066X.41.9.954.

169 **Dr. Pauline Boss coined the phrase:** Pauline Boss, "The
Trauma and Complicated Grief of Ambiguous Loss." *Pastoral
Psychology* 52, no. 2 (November 2009): 137–45; doi: 10.1007/
s11089-009-0264-0.

170 **"Creative individuals are childlike":** Mihaly Csikszentmihalyi,
Creativity: Flow and the Psychology of Discovery and Invention (New York:
HarperCollins, 1996), 346.

170 **"Do not try to do extraordinary things":** Emily Carr, *Hundreds
and Thousands: The Journals of Emily Carr* (Vancover: Douglas &
McIntyre, 2006).

175 **"The Buddhists say":** Offill, *Dept. of Speculation,* 47.

175 **"It happens through some combination":** Pema Chödrön,
*Comfortable with Uncertainty: 108 Teachings on Cultivating Fearlessness and
Compassion* (Boston: Shambhala, 2003), 81.

176 **"Spiritual awakening is frequently described":** Chödrön,
Comfortable with Uncertainty, 1.

177 **"We have a concept of ourselves":** Pema Chödrön, *When Things
Fall Apart: Heart Advice for Difficult Times* (London: Thorsons Classics,
2017), 58, 68.

179 **"What we learn from experience":** Phillips, *Missing Out,* 161.

179 **"don't know anything"**: Chödrön, *When Things Fall Apart*, 12.

179 **"We already have everything we need"**: Pema Chödrön, *Start Where You Are: A Guide to Compassionate Living* (Boston: Shambhala, 2001), 1.

180 **"Who ever got the idea"**: Chödrön, *When Things Fall Apart*, 78–79.

180 **"Start taking off"**: Chödrön, *Comfortable with Uncertainty*, 112.

181 **"What kind of pleasures"**: Phillips, *Missing Out*, xv.

Chapter 8: I Danced Myself Out of the Womb

191 *"The Internet is nothing like a cigarette break"*: Shapiro, *Still Writing*, 159.

193 **You don't have to dig:** "Creativity." Wikipedia, January 17, 2019; https://en.wikipedia.org/wiki/Creativity.

194 **In fact, these days around half of all Americans:** *A Decade of Arts Engagement: Findings from the Survey of Public Participation in the Arts, 2002–2012.* National Endowment for the Arts, NEA Research Report No. 58, 2015.

194 **Carrie Battan wrote about this in *The New Yorker*:** Carrie Battan, "'The Artist's Way' in an Age of Self-Promotion." *The New Yorker,* May 4, 2016; https://www.newyorker.com/culture/cultural -comment/the-artists-way-in-an-age-of-self-promotion.

196 *everyday creativity:* Ruth Richards, "Everyday Creativity: Process and Way of Life—Four Key Issues." In *The Cambridge Handbook of Creativity*, ed. James Kaufman and Robert Sternberg (New York: Cambridge University Press, 2010), 189–215.

200 **"I mean all human beings":** Virginia Woolf, *Moments of Being* (New York: Harvest Books, 1985), 72.

201 **"nodding terms":** Didion, *Slouching Towards Bethlehem.*

Chapter 9: The Ghost Ship That Didn't Carry Us

205 **"a melodic gesture":** "The Impact of Barber's 'Adagio for Strings.'" NPR, November 4, 2006; https://www.npr.org/2006/11/04/6427815 /the-impact-of-barbers-adagio-for-strings.

212 **"I think that . . . most of us would not want to trade":** Todd May, "If You Could Be Someone Else, Would You?" *The New York*

Times, July 17, 2017; https://www.nytimes.com/2017/07/17/opinion /if-you-could-be-someone-else-would-you.html.

213 **"haunted by the myth of our potential":** Phillips, *Missing Out,* xi, xiii.

213 **"I was so busy wanting to be Julia Roberts":** Clay Skipper, "Sarah Paulson's Career Advice? Don't Succeed Early." *GQ,* September 18, 2016; https://www.gq.com/story/unexpected-sarah -paulson.

216 **a beautiful memoir by Glenn Kurtz:** Glenn Kurtz, *Practicing: A Musician's Return to Music* (New York: Vintage Books, 2008).